THE
UNTAMED
Tongue

THE
UNTAMED
Tongue

A DISSENTING DICTIONARY

THOMAS SZASZ

Open ✸ Court
La Salle, Illinois

Front cover illustration: *The Angel Michael Binding Satan*, circa 1805, by William Blake: watercolor, black ink, and graphite. Courtesy of The Fogg Art Museum, Harvard University, Cambridge, Massachusetts. Gift of W. A. White.

OPEN COURT and the above logo are registered in the U.S. Patent and Trademark Office.

© 1990 by Open Court Publishing Company

First printing 1990
Second printing 1991

Printed and bound in the United States of America.

Library of Congress Cataloging-in-Publication Data

Szasz, Thomas Stephen, 1920–
   The untamed tongue: a dissenting dictionary/Thomas Szasz.
     p. cm.
   ISBN 0-8126-9103-2. –ISBN 0-8126-9104-0 (pbk.)
   1. Aphorisms and apothegms. I. Title.
PN6269.A2S95   1990   90-7543
818' .5402–dc20   CIP

For every kind of beast and bird, of reptile and sea creature, can be tamed and has been tamed by humankind, but no human being can tame the tongue — a restless evil, full of poison.

—JAMES, 3:7–8*

Contents

Preface

Salvation, piety, power, love of God or country, money, fame, sex, procreation, health, happiness, peace of mind, honest and useful labor, helping the poor and oppressed: is there a common denominator among these diverse aspirations that men and women have viewed as the ultimate aim of life? The quest for legitimacy seems to be such a common demoninator: Everyone tries to legitimize his existence — to himself, his parents, his peers, the pillars of society, posterity, God. Indeed, for us human beings, the struggle for legitimacy seems to be as elementary and indispensable as is, for non-human animals, the struggle for life itself.

How, then, do we gain or lose legitimacy? In the Age of Faith men gained and lost it by pleasing and displeasing God. In those days — bygone for many of us, resurrected or never relinquished by others — only God was unconditionally legitimate. All else in the universe was legitimate only if its existence pleased Him and accorded with His will. If it did not, whatever it was — man or beast or inanimate object — was illegitimate and hence unworthy of existence. Since God was the Grand Legitimizer, nothing was more important than divining and faithfully observing His will.

Having decided that God is dead, where does modern man locate the ultimate source of legitimacy — in particular, the legitimacy of human behavior? Since ours is the Age of Reason, our ultimate source of legitimacy is Science. Beliefs about the behavior of non-human animals, plants, and inanimate objects, governed by the laws of biology, chemistry, and physics, must be legitimated by the Natural or Positive Sciences; while beliefs about the behavior of human beings, (supposedly) governed by the laws of economics, psychology, and sociology, must be legitimated by the Social Sciences. Hence our blind reliance on the doctrines of the Behavioral — or, as Jacques Barzun has aptly dubbed them, Misbehavioral — Sciences;[1] and hence, too, our fanatical faith in the ministrations of the minions of the so-called helping — but actually, hindering — professions.

While many entries in this dictionary refer to ideas and interventions formally recognized as falling within the provinces of psychiatry, psychology, or the social sciences, many do not. In either case, each is an observation about or comment on some aspect of the human condition, as I see it. I should like to add that not only are my remarks not inspired by what now passes as knowledge revealed by the Misbehavioral Sciences, but, on the contrary, they are stimulated by that simple spirit of dissent which Camus captured so perfectly in *The Plague*: "But again and again, there comes a time in history when the man who dares to say that two and two make four is punished with death."[2] Even if such a man no longer runs the risk of being punished with literal death, surely he still runs the risk of being punished with metaphorical death — that is, with loss of legitimacy.

Most of the material in this volume appears here for the first time. Some of the entries are reprinted, many in revised form, from my two previous collections of aphorisms — *The Second Sin* and *Heresies* — both of which have been out of print for some time.

I wish to thank David Ramsay Steele for his critical comments and constructive editorial suggestions; and, once again, my daughter, Suzy, and my brother, George, for their devoted help.

INTRODUCTION

Serious error would seem to require serious argument to refute it. While this may be true in the hard sciences which deal with material objects, it is not true in the social sciences which deal with human affairs. Indeed, faced with the pretentious solemnity of official Nonsense, evidence and reason are helpless. Our only effective weapon against it is laughter, especially the laughter of ridicule. "Nothing," observed Voltaire, "is so effective in crushing superstition as mockery. . . . Ridicule gets the better of anything; it is the most powerful of weapons."[1]

Familiar to the classical world, satire virtually vanished during the Age of Faith, that is, from the fourth to the sixteenth century. The New Testament foreshadows Christianity's distrust of laughter and levity. "Let your laughter be turned to mourning," preaches James, "and your joy to dejection."[2] Trying to stem the renaissance of laughter, Francis Bacon inveighs (in 1597): "As for Jest, there are certain things which ought to be privileged from it: namely, Religion, Matters of State, Great Persons."[3]

In his majestic work on Rabelais, Mikhail Bakhtin reminds us that "Early Christianity had already condemned laughter. . . . John Chrysostom declared that jest and laughter are not from God but from the devil."[4] Rabelais rejected this and reclaimed laughter by attributing divine legitimacy to it:

> God who subjected the world to man,
> To man alone permitted laughter
> To be merry, not to the beast
> Who has neither reason nor spirit.[5]

To be sure, the Official—abstractly as Truth, or concretely as Very Important Person or Institution—still demands seriousness. This is hardly surprising. After all, who are the eternal enemies of tolerance and truth? Their official guardians: Church and State, and—in our day—Science and Medicine. In their zeal for ideological hegemony—for dominion over the soul and mind and body of man—the oracles who speak in the name of God, Country, Science, or Health practice not only fraud and force, but also demand awe and deference. In their presence, toward their profundities, solemnity is the only proper sentiment: laughter is intolerable, ridicule is sacrilege.

The Church's demand for solemnity, no less than its demand for stupidity, had to be repudiated before man could turn his interest from heaven and hell to heavenly and earthly bodies. We regard Copernicus (1473–1543) as the man who successfully repudiated religious thought-control, epitomized by the Church's control over cosmology; and ought to regard Rabelais (c. 1494–1553) as the man who successfully repudiated religious mood-control, epitomized by the Church's control over laughter. Indeed, as Bakhtin emphasizes, the history of laughter is an important chapter in the history of man's liberation from hypocrisy, stupidity, and oppression:

> Laughter liberates not only from external censorship, but first of all from the great interior censor; it liberates from . . . fear of the sacred, of prohibitions, of the past, of power . . . . Seriousness had an official tone . . . It oppressed, frightened, bound, lied, and wore the mask of hypocrisy. . . . Thus, distrust of the serious tone and confidence in the trust of laughter had a spontaneous, elemental character.[6]

Of course, the subjects I address in this volume are serious and their duly appointed officials speak in the solemn tones appropriate to their lofty positions. But I agree with Voltaire when he said: "I look on solemnity as a disease! It seems to me that morality, study and gaiety are three sisters which should never be separated."[7]

Let us never forget that the guardians must themselves be guarded, especially against taking themselves too seriously. If they cannot laugh at themselves, they deserve to have us laugh at them. In fact, we fail to do so at our own peril.

CHILDREN AND PARENTS

A child becomes an adult when he realizes that he has a right not only to be right but also to be wrong.

Control communicates care and devotion to children, condescension and disdain to adults. Herein lies a fundamental dilemma of society: It ought to encourage parents to love and control their children, and politicians to respect their fellow citizens and leave them alone.

Modern societies are well on their way to inverting this arrangement: They encourage parents to fake respect for their children and thus justify their failure to control them; and politicians to fake love for their fellow citizens and thus justify their efforts to exercise capricious control over them.

Because children cannot accomplish as much as adults, they are usually rewarded for effort. But they must be taught that what counts in life is not effort but achievement. If children are over-rewarded for effort, they may continue to seek approval solely for trying instead of for succeeding. This dooms them to failure; for if they succeed, they succeed only at trying hard; and if they fail, they fail dismally.

The two tasks of youth: developing self-discipline and acquiring marketable skills.

Excepting suicide, the most serious decision in life should be to have a child; however, not to have a child, if one is capable of having children, should perhaps be an even more serious decision.

Although it is hard for a son to compete with a successful father, it may be even harder for him to compete with an unsuccessful one. This is because most young men find the prospect of their own failure easier to bear than the prospect of being the instruments of their fathers' humiliation.

Parents teach children discipline for two different, indeed diametrically opposite, reasons: to render the child submissive to them and to make him independent of them. Only a self-disciplined person can be obedient; and only such a person can be autonomous.

Some parents want their children to *have it* better, others want them to *do* better. The former are likely to have incompetent and unhappy children, the latter, competent and happy ones.

Why do children want to grow up? Because they experience their lives as constrained by immaturity and perceive adulthood as a condition of greater freedom and opportunity. But what is there today, in America, that very poor and very rich adolescents want to do but cannot do? Not much: They can *do* drugs, *have* sex, *make* babies, and *get* money (from their parents, crime, or the State). For such adolescents, adulthood becomes synonymous with responsibility rather than liberty. Is it any surprise that they remain adolescents?

Formerly, when parents couldn't cope with their children, they enlisted relatives to discipline them or hired governesses and tutors to do so. Now, they abuse them or hire child psychiatrists and mental hospitals to do so.

In the past, parents and psychiatrists tortured sexually active (masturbating) children with mechanical restraints. Today, they torture hyperactive children with chemical restraints (psychoactive drugs).

The moral: Only adults and drugs are allowed to be active (children should be seen, not heard).

As a parent, perhaps the most important message you

must convey to your daughter or son is: 'Listen to your inner voice and trust it. Listen to and learn from others but never let them undermine your confidence in your own judgment.' Of course, you won't be able to do so unless you yourself believe it, and act accordingly.

Juvenile court judges now routinely send children deemed to be 'ungovernable' or 'in need of supervision' to psychiatrists. The child, reasonably enough, views the psychiatrist so imposed on him as his adversary rather than his ally. The psychiatrist who 'sees' such a child insists on viewing himself as the protector of the child's best interests. The parents and juvenile court judges who initiate this process insist on viewing themselves as helping the child get the 'treatment' he needs. If we wanted to hasten the destruction of children injured by parental neglect, it would be difficult to devise a more effective mechanism for doing so.

In the universe of persons, children rank first both as the most wanted and the most unwanted. Depending on the child's age and the society by whose rules his parents must guide themselves, there are about a half dozen ways in which the latter can, legally, get rid of the former. Some of these methods of disposing of unwanted children are even considered to be socially praiseworthy. Thus, the fetus may be disposed of by abortion; the infant, by adoption or infanticide; the older child, by adoption or confinement in an orphanage; the adolescent and the adult child, by confinement in a mental hospital (and by further destruction of his self there, by sterilization, electro-shock, lobotomy, or anti-psychotic drugs).

In the United States today there is a pervasive tendency to treat children as adults, and adults as children. The options of children are thus steadily expanded, while those of adults are progressively constricted. The result is unruly children and childish adults.

Disease

A glossary:

Disease: 1. Proven bodily lesion. 2. Putative bodily lesion. 3. Distress, disability, disadvantage, dysfunction. 4. An (ostensibly) treatable condition. 5. Irrationality. 6. Irresponsibility. 7. Crime. 8. Any human behavior or characteristic we dislike.

Treatment: 1. Intervention sought by a patient from a physician for the amelioration or cure of disease. 2. Punishment (as in 'Let's give him the treatment . . . '; especially popular in psychiatric institutions and totalitarian countries).

Bad habits treated as diseases:

Using alcohol badly is called 'alcoholism' and is treated with Antabuse.

Using food badly is called 'anorexia nervosa' or 'obesity'; the former is treated with electroshock, the latter with amphetamines or intestinal bypass operations.

Using sex badly is called 'perversion', and is treated with

electrical stimulation through electrodes implanted in the brain and with sex-change operations.

Using language badly is called 'psychosis' and is treated with anti-psychotic drugs.

The term 'illness' can mean either a disease (lesion) or the state of feeling sick (a sense of being ill or unwell). In the former case, 'illness' is synonymous with 'disease'; this is indeed the way these two terms are used in everyday speech. In the latter case, 'illness' is an abstract noun without material or objective referent; in this sense, there is no difference between saying 'I feel ill' and saying 'I have an illness'. Notice, however, that *feeling ill* is analogous to *feeling well*, or *happy*, or *sad*; but that it would be nonsensical to replace these expressions with *I have a wellness*, or *I have a happiness*, or *I have a sadness*.

In short, 'I feel sick/ill' is what we say when we feel indisposed—because of disease or some other reason. Accordingly, feeling ill may or may not be a reason for assuming the sick role and seeking medical help.

Demonstrable bodily lesion is the gold standard of medical diagnosis. Without practical convertibility into gold, the value of paper money rests only on faith. Without conceptual convertibility into bodily lesion, the diagnosis of disease rests only on faith. Unbacked by gold, paper money is *fiat* money—the politically irresistible incentive for debauching the currency, called 'inflation'. Unbacked by lesion, diagnosis is *fiat* diagnosis — the medically irresistible incentive for debauching the concept of disease, called 'psychiatry'.

Today, disease is largely a *strategic category*. If the (American) government classifies a pattern of behavior — say, drug (ab)use — as *behavior*, then it cannot regulate it. That is why, when the government tries to regulate *behavior* — for example, the right to smoke in private — we indignantly protest: 'But this is a free country!'

However, if the government can classify a pattern of behavior as an *illness* — for example, 'alcoholism' — then it can regulate 'it' by appealing to its powerful impact on business, health, economics, and so forth.

Finally, if the government can classify a pattern of behavior as a (serious) *mental illness* — for example, 'schizophrenia' — then it can directly regulate personal behavior itself, by depriving the individual of the right to free speech, property, and liberty.

Seemingly oblivious to all this, jurists, psychologists, physicians, and scientists continue to debate whether X is or is not a disease.

"October 2 through 8 is Mental Illness Awareness Week, part of an ongoing effort by the American Psychiatric Association to 'reduce the stigma surrounding mental illnesses', including schizophrenia . . . Many social scientists say that one factor that tends to destigmatize a disorder is defining it as a medical problem . . . "[1]

The American Psychiatric Association thus acknowledges that, ostensibly in an effort to destigmatize stigmatized (mis)behavior, it accepts such an ostensibly noble motive as a legitimate ground for counting stigmatized (mis)behavior as disease. However, this self-flattering posture evades confronting the question of whether it is desirable or undesirable to destigmatize behavior such as was exhibited by, say, John Hinckley, Jr., currently the most famous 'schizophrenic' in the United States.

In the case of bodily illness, the patient pays, or is willing to pay, the doctor to relieve him of (being bothered by) his illness; in the case of mental illness, we (the taxpayers) pay, and are willing to pay, the psychiatrist to relieve us of (being bothered by) the patient.

A Canadian politician has discovered a new disease: illiteracy. Declares Senator Joyce Fairbairn (Ontario): "Honorable senators, illiteracy touches probably more than 20 percent of our population. . . . It is not a partisan issue. It affects us all . . . [it] is truly a national disease . . . [We] must understand that this is one disease that can be cured."[2] Spreading the alarm, a reporter (from Ottawa) adds: "Illiterates more commonly read the Bible and other religious material, while literates lean more to reference books, fiction, and manuals."[3]

Question: Who is illiterate?

Formerly, people had strong sexual desires or needs and were responsible for controlling them; now they suffer from the disease of 'sex addiction'. "Evangelist Jimmy Swaggart, who paid prostitutes to perform lewd sex acts, is one of 10 million Americans suffering from an addiction . . . ," asserts David M. Moss, director of the Coventry Association for Pastoral Psychology in Atlanta. Victor B. Cline, a clinical psychologist at the University of Utah, agrees: "I see Swaggart as a good man but he had a secret illness going back to his teens."[4]

Jennifer Schneider, M.D., a specialist in internal medicine, asserts that "repeated sexual affairs may signal addictive behavior. . . . my husband admitted he had love affairs . . . He said he couldn't control his behavior." Mr. Schneider was cured in "a program for sexual addicts modeled after Alcoholics Anonymous". Dr. Schneider recommends four such organizations: "SA (Sexaholics Anonymous), CoSA (for Co-dependents of Sex Addicts), SLAA (Sex and Love Addicts Anonymous), and SAA (Sex Addicts Anonymous)."[5]

"Compulsive gambling is a damaging disease for an

estimated nine million Americans," asserts Amin Daghestani, professor of psychiatry at Loyola University in Chicago. "Physicians everywhere must recognize this problem as a treatable, medical condition."[6]

"Chronic gambling," we read in the *New York Times*, may be a chemically caused illness:

> The psychological forces that propel so many chronic gamblers to ruin marriages, lose jobs, and even turn to crime may spring from a biological need . . . . the biological findings suggest that pathological gamblers suffer from an addiction like alcoholism . . . gamblers had lower levels than usual of the brain chemicals that regulate arousal . . . they may engage in activities like gambling to increase their levels of these chemicals in the noradrenergic system, which secretes them.[7]

Evidently, I have been mistaken: I have always thought that a pathological gambler was a gambler who lost money, not his wife; and that people gambled not because they wanted to increase the levels of certain chemicals in their brains, but because they enjoyed gambling and hoped to win.

Lionel Solursh, professor of psychiatry at the Medical College of Georgia, has discovered a new disease; "Combat Addiction". Supposedly occurring mainly in "intoxicant abusers and violence-addicted veterans," the diagnosis of this disease rests solely on the metaphors used by the (so-called) patients to describe their (alleged) experiences:

> . . . the rush or the feeling that you get from this is one of an addiction to adrenalin, addiction to cocaine . . . when I get into this

high it is just like being in Vietnam, the thrill of killing, the thrill
of destroying. And it's something I just cannot overcome, even
with medication. . . . It's hard to duplicate this high with drugs,
except the only drug I know is cocaine . . . [that gives you] the
same type of high of killing, of destroying.[8]

Discovery of the disease manifested by the thrill of
mugging, stealing, cheating, and lying must be right around
the corner, requiring only more funding for psychiatric
research.

Fact #1: Psychiatrists now maintain that the drug abuser
and the pathological gambler are sick and need treatment.

Fact #2: Persons so afflicted pay for their 'illness', but
not for its treatment. (Such patients have no trouble finding
the money for drugs or wagering, but seem never to have
any money for treatment for drug abuse or pathological
gambling.)

Fact #3: The psychiatrist treating such patients is paid
by the State, which gives him a vested economic interest in
the State's defining personal irresponsibility as impersonal
illness.

New models of mental illnesses are now produced faster
than new models of automobiles, perhaps because they sell
faster. A new Italian model is "art sickness" or the "Stendhal
Syndrome":

In a 182-page book titled 'The Stendhal Syndrome', [Dr.
Graziella] Magherini details the cases of 106 tourists admitted to

Santa Maria Nuova Hospital in Florence in the last 10 years suffering from delirium, disorientation and paranoia brought on by
exposure to magnificent works of art. Hundreds of milder cases,
probably thousands more, have gone unreported. . . . "The worst
case had to be in the hospital 10 days," said Magherini, head of
the psychiatric ward at Santa Maria Nuova and a lecturer on
psychiatry at the University of Florence.[9]

"A sucker is born every minute," observed Phineas Bar-
num. Now the suckers are called 'mental patients' (who
believe they are sick) and 'health insurers' (who pay for the
fictitious treatments of non-existent illnesses).

Here is a recently discovered disease so ridiculous it
defies being ridiculed:

Psychiatrists and psychologists at Hartgrove Hospital [in
Chicago] . . . are creating one of the nation's first treatment programs to wean teen-agers away from Satanism. . . . "I don't think
there is any doubt Satanism is a growing problem," said social
worker Dale Trahan, who has been researching Satanic beliefs for
three years and was contracted to organize the program for the
Treatment of Ritualistic Deviance. . . . In the program, teen-agers
will spend four to eight weeks as in-patients and undergo individual and group counseling. . . . The new program will seek to
undermine Satanism's underlying belief system. . . .[10]

The concept of disease is fast replacing the concept of
responsibility. With increasing zeal Americans use and interpret the assertion 'I am sick' as equivalent to the assertion
'I am not responsible': Smokers say they are not responsible
for smoking, drinkers that they are not responsible for
drinking, gamblers that they are not responsible for gam-

bling, and mothers who murder their infants that they are not responsible for killing. To prove their point — and to capitalize on their self-destructive and destructive behavior — smokers, drinkers, gamblers, and insanity acquittees are suing tobacco companies, liquor companies, gambling casinos, and physicians.

Can American society survive this legal-psychiatric assault on its moral and political foundations?

It is senseless to debate whether alcoholism or kleptomania are or are not diseases. The fact that we call drinking 'too often' or 'too much' alcoholism, and stealing things the thief 'does not need' kleptomania are symptoms of our belief that they are diseases and of our desire to treat them as such. If we wanted to seriously consider how we ought to classify, understand, and respond to such behaviors we would have to name them in ways that do not prejudge their medical or moral character — which is virtually impossible.

DRUGS

No drug can expand consciousness: the only thing a drug can expand is the earnings of the company that makes it.

The FDA calls certain substances 'controlled'. But there are no controlled substances; there are only controlled persons.

Drug laws are our dietary laws: Doctors are our rabbis; heroin, our pork; addicts, our unclean persons.

Treating addiction to heroin with methadone is like treating addiction to scotch with bourbon.

Giving oneself addictive drugs is a crime. Accepting addictive drugs from a 'maintenance program' is a treatment.

Possessing hypodermic needles without a prescription is a crime. Accepting hypodermic needles from the state without a prescription is a treatment.

It is legal to burn the American flag in public, but it is illegal to smoke an American marijuana cigarette in private.

Years ago, when Judaism in Spain was prohibited and Catholicism promoted, many Jews became Catholics. This was called 'conversion'. Today, when heroin in the United States is prohibited and methadone promoted, many heroin addicts become methadone addicts. We call this 'treatment'.

Making drugs legal does not make them more toxic, but making them illegal does, because the distributors of illegal drugs adulterate their product (and have no competitor who sells the same product in unadulterated form).

The Nazis had a Jewish problem. We have a drug abuse problem. Actually, 'Jewish problem' was the name the Germans gave to their persecution of the Jews; 'drug abuse problem' is the name we give to our persecution of people who use certain drugs.

Some experts now advocate that heroin be prohibited;

others, that it be given free to addicts. Why should heroin be prohibited when alcohol and cigarettes are not? Why should heroin be dispensed at the taxpayer's expense to those who crave it, when alcohol and cigarettes are not? It is revealing of our propensity for medical meddling that every conceivable intervention in the lives of addicts is now seriously advocated and widely supported, save one: repealing all anti-drug laws and leaving so-called addicts alone.

Formerly, had Americans demanded that farmers in a foreign country grow or not grow certain crops, it would have been called colonialism and been vigorously opposed by patriots abroad and Liberals at home. Now when they demand precisely this, it is called narcotics control, and is enthusiastically supported by patriots abroad and both Liberals and Conservatives at home. For dishonored and dishonorable religious and military colonialisms we have thus substituted an honored and honorable medical colonialism.

American politicians denounce foreign 'drug lords' for exporting certain mind-altering substances to the United States. However, these substances—for example, cocaine or heroin—are correctly identified for what they are: Americans who want to buy them know what they are getting; and no one is forced to expose himself unknowingly or against his will to the potentially harmful effects of these substances. In short, every American can easily protect himself from the risk of such foreign substances by simply avoiding them.

At the same time, American politicians defend the right of American companies to export not only alcohol and tobacco to foreign countries, but also toxic wastes. Typically, these wastes are dumped in the soil and waters of foreign (usually Third World) countries. The inhabitants of those countries do not know what dangerous substances are being imported; where they are stored or what they have contaminated; hence they cannot, by any individual action on their part, protect themselves from being poisoned by such toxic waste. The profits from this business are, not surprisingly, enormous. "If I'm exporting [waste]," says one trader in toxic waste, "I can just say, "So, I'm immoral.' " The reporters for *Newsweek* add: "For, unlike the trade in drugs . . . dumping poison in poor countries is perfectly legal."[1]

Drug prohibition is unwise social policy for many reasons, most obviously because forbidden fruit tastes sweeter: that is, because one of the easiest ways for a person (especially a young person) to assert his autonomy is by defying authority (especially arbitrary and hypocritical authority).

Centuries ago in the Christian West, usury was both a great personal sin and a social danger. Why? Because the usurer tempted the would-be money-user. Today, especially in the United States, drug trafficking has replaced usury. Why? Because the drug pusher tempts the would-be drug-user. The idea that it is a grave moral wrong to treat money as a commodity generated the illicit trade in money; similarly, the idea that it is a grave moral wrong to treat

drugs as a commodity now generates the illicit trade in
drugs.

The principal (often the only) victims of drug (ab)use
are the persons who use drugs; whereas the principal (often
the only) victims of the War on Drugs are the persons who
do not use (or deal in) drugs. Herein — that is, in placing
higher value on protecting people from themselves than on
protecting them from each other (and the government) —
lies the ultimate immorality and injustice of anti-drug laws.

Ostensibly, the use of illicit drugs, such as cocaine or
heroin, is prohibited because they impair the social functioning of the person who uses them. This claim is inconsis-
tent with the fact that the authorities — parents, politicians,
and physicians — don't know who uses such drugs, and support costly efforts to develop and deploy tests to find illicit
users. If illicit drugs really impaired social functioning — a
contingency clearly absurd without specifying drugs and
dosages — then we would need no special tests to identify
the users. And if they don't impair social functioning — which is often clearly the case — then testing people for
drug abuse by examining their blood or urine is unlike
testing them for a disease and, instead, is like entrapping
them into incriminating themselves as criminals.

In the United States today, the most important social
function of the anti-drug hysteria is that it conceals racial
animosities as a problem of drug abuse, and converts a

potentially violent race war into an ostensibly therapeutic War on Drugs. The second most important function of the anti-drug hysteria is that it provides bread and circuses for the uneducated, unemployed, and unwanted non-white urban youth.

Accomplished American actors and athletes, who exercise superlative control over their bodies, are now often paraded before us as victims of an insidious illness that utterly robs them of their ability to control their craving for drugs. These persons — now viewed as patients suffering from a disease called 'substance abuse disorder' — are usually guilty of no less than four of the seven deadly sins: lust, pride, gluttony, and greed. Of course, if we insist on idolizing morally imperfect crooners and gladiators, then we must deny their moral imperfections.

We are now told that medical evidence is accumulating that the disposition to drink alcohol to excess may be partly genetically determined. If this is true, then an individual informed that he is genetically so disposed becomes, *ipso facto*, more, not less, responsible than others not so affected for learning to control his drinking or to abstain from alcohol altogether.

Addiction-mongers used to base their claim that drinking and smoking are diseases on the fact that such behaviors cause diseases, such as cirrhosis of the liver and cancer of the lung. No more. Emboldened by their successes, they now insist that family members who abstain from such drugs but fail to denounce their drug-using relatives to medical authorities are also sick, suffering from 'co-dependence': "Rather than confront addicts, co-dependents cover for them . . . [exhibiting] 'irrational endurance' or 'enabling behavior'. One woman's daughter lent her father her lunch money. . . . Co-dependents have their own version of denial."[2]

Suppose the daughter of a man with angina or cancer colludes with her father in denying his illness and avoiding treatment for it; does that make her 'co-anginal' or 'co-cancerous'?

Americans are now free to buy guns and bullets, but not syringes and drugs. To me, this suggests that we are more afraid of injecting ourselves with a drug than of being shot by an assailant with a bullet; that we are more afraid of shooting ourselves metaphorically than of being shot literally by someone else; in short, that we are more afraid of ourselves than of our enemies.

Today, persons often go to doctors — especially to family physicians and psychiatrists — for only one purpose, namely, to obtain a prescription for a drug they cannot buy without it. Such a patient is like a small child who wants a cookie but is unable to get into the cookie jar; the cookie jar being the pharmacy; the cookie, the 'controlled substance'; and the parent doling out the cookies, the physician.

If a person takes a drug prescribed for him by a

psychiatrist and claims that it makes him feel better, that proves mental illness is a bona fide disease; but if he takes a drug prohibited for him by legislators and claims that it makes him feel better, that proves he is an addict.

Ideally, medical practice rests on two premises: first, that the patient has an objectively demonstrable abnormal condition of his body; second, that he and his physician co-operate in an effort to control or cure the disease. With respect to so-called drug abuse, neither of these premises obtains: the (alleged) diseases are actually patterns of actions or habits (which, of course, may result in bodily diseases); and the (alleged) patients do not, as a rule, seek medical help. Hence, the relationship addicts form with their doctors or other therapists, which usually come into being as a result of external coercion, are fragile and likely to be mutually antagonistic rather than co-operative.

Before 1914, a person could buy and use a drug (any drug) because he *wanted* to; he did not have to prove to anyone that he *needed* it. He can still buy and use a cane (or crutch) if he *wants* to; he does not have to prove to anyone that he *needs* it.

Today, we are increasingly denied the right to buy and use drugs because we want them; instead, we must first prove to a physician that we need a particular drug; and even then we may not be able to obtain it because, increasingly, physicians too have to demonstrate to authorities, who sit in judgment on them, that *they need* to prescribe that drug.

The Romans believed that in wine there is truth ('in vino veritas'): Under the influence of alcohol people will say and do things that they otherwise try to conceal. We believe that in wine there is lunacy: Under the influence of alcohol people will say and do things that are out of character and non-volitional. Such behavior is believed to be 'caused' by the drug and is viewed as unrelated to the actor as moral agent. Is this an advance or a retrogression in the understanding of the nature of man? In psychology? In psychiatry as (ostensibly) the biosocial science of man?

The more enthusiastically we transform the drug market from being based on wants ('I want X, am willing to pay for X, hence can buy X'), to being based on needs ('I need X, am willing to beg for it from a physician, hence am entitled to receive it free from the State'), the more stupidly and swiftly we march down the road to a serfdom unanticipated by Adam Smith or even Friedrich Hayek.

A hundred years ago, a person could legally purchase — in the free market — all the pure and safe opium he wanted. Today, he can illegally purchase — on the black market and for a large sum — a negligible amount of impure and unsafe opiate. This is where the anticapitalist mentality combined with the therapeutic ethic have brought us.

Predictably, the War on Drugs has failed to curb the use of illegal drugs; however, it has succeeded in obliterating, in the public mind, an elementary distinction concerning self-medication. Thomas Jefferson used legal opium to preserve his life. John Belushi used illegal 'drugs' to destroy his. Like any behavior, self-medication may be disciplined and self-preservative or undisciplined and self-destructive. Most (illegal) drug use, like the use of most other things, is, of course, neither self-preservative nor self-destructive.

We, Americans, are supposed to be endowed with in-alienable rights. In fact, none of us has any rights at all unless they are supported by a 'lobby'. Blacks, women, homosexuals, defense contractors, farmers, the old, the handicapped, persons for and against abortion, alcohol, tobacco, gambling, and guns, all have lobbies protecting their rights. In contrast, when blacks, women, and homo-sexuals had no lobby — they had no rights; during the Second World War, Japanese-Americans had no lobby — and no rights; during the War on Drugs that has been rag-ing for the past three decades, 'drug abusers' and 'drug pushers' have had no lobby — and have no rights. So long as the very idea of a cocaine or heroin lobby seems absurd to Americans — as absurd as, say, a lobby for the rights of polygamists — there can be no end to the War on Drugs.

The person whose ability to move his muscles is im-paired — by injury, illness or old age — uses a cane or crutch. The person whose ability to live his life is impaired — by ideas, memories, or social circumstances — uses drugs. As the crutch helps a person to move his limbs better, so the drug helps him to live his life better — 'better' being defined, in each case, by the subject himself. If the market in canes were criminalized; that is, if canes could be obtained legally only with a physician's prescription (preferably requiring a triplicate form, so that the physician's own prescribing habits could be properly monitored); or if they could be obtained only illegally, in the black market—many people would probably feel deprived of canes and would acquire the habit of using them.

Would outlawing condoms stop people from engaging in illicit sexual acts? Obviously not. Did outlawing hypodermic syringes and needles stop people from using illicit drugs? No. The result: The single most important source for the transmission of AIDS in America today is the use of illegal syringes and needles.

The Soviet government censors the press; hence, the Russians have a *samizdat* (underground) press—which American presidents interpret as proof of the spiritual invincibility of the free market. The American government censors 'substances' (drugs); hence, the Americans have a *samizdat* (underground) pharmacopoeia—which American presidents interpret as proof of the subversion of the free market by greedy 'drug lords' and hostile foreign governments.

Mrs. Reagan enjoined us to "Just Say No!" to drugs. To make sure we did, Mr. Reagan promised to punish us harshly if we said yes. This fradulent choice epitomizes the ugliness of American political paternalism. Wouldn't it have been more ethical, more elegant, and also more effective if President and Mrs. Reagan, as well as other politicians, had said to us: 'You have a right to use drugs but that doesn't mean it's right that you do so'?

A policeman is killed in New York City, allegedly by drug traffickers. In a full-page ad in the *New York Times*, Mayor Ed Koch eulogizes the victim in these words:

> The executioner will be hunted down and prosecuted . . . [but] that will treat the symptom, not the disease. The disease is drug trafficking, a cancer to which no community is immune. Its practitioners are the most nefarious of criminals . . . The cure will be found several thousand miles from Queens—in places like Mexico, Panama . . .[3]

Drug trafficking is a disease. Can one practice a disease? Can the practitioner of a disease be a criminal? Can coercing and killing the peaceful citizens of sovereign foreign nations be a cure? If Jefferson were alive, perhaps he would now say: 'I tremble for my country when I think that God cares about the truth.'

Consistency is not one of Mayor Koch's (or any demagogic politician's) strong suits. Only three days after his hysterical expostulations about drug controls he turns his gaze on welfare and writes: "There is a limit to what government can and should do in a democracy. No city or state can be expected to protect adults from themselves."[4] But what was the unfortunate policeman killed by drug traffickers doing if not protecting adults from themselves? After all, no New Yorker *has* to patronize drug traffickers.

On March 28, 1988, under the title 'Candidates' Survival Guide', *Newsweek* magazine ran a condensed summary of "How they make it to the next photo opportunity." Listing Democrats and Republicans in alphabetical order, the table supplied information on eight items: "Road food; Entertainment; Exercise; Medication; Sleep; Naps; Media techniques; and Campaign ambience." For future historians of America's Holy War on Drugs, I herewith list the entries[5] under "Medication" (exactly as printed):

Michael Dukakis: "a glass of white wine, as often as once a week."

Richard Gephardt: "occasional beer."

Albert Gore: "none."

Jesse Jackson: "doesn't smoke or drink; occasional aspirin."

Paul Simon: "none."

George Bush: "occasional Margarita or vodka martini at end of day."

Bob Dole: "occasional half glass of white wine."

Pat Robertson: "none."

Note that: 1. beer, wine, and cocktails are listed under "Medication", with aspirin; 2. for Jesse Jackson, *not* smoking or drinking is listed as a medication; 3. three out of eight candidates claim not to use any medication at all; 4.

none of the candidates smokes (or admits it); 5. only one candidate, Bush, acknowledges drinking hard liquor.

In the Age of Faith, people demonstrated their love of God and of their fellow man by forcibly converting the heathen and by extolling, as holy, religious coercion. Today, in the Age of Therapy, people demonstrate their love of Health and of their fellow man by forcibly treating the sick and by extolling, as noble, therapeutic coercion. A full-page ad in *Newsweek* magazine carries this headline: "Sometimes, the worst thing you can do to a drug user is the only way to help." Sponsored by the "Partnership for a Drug Free America", the ad invites readers to call the "National Institute on Drug Abuse hot line."[6] "If any one slay with the sword," warns the Bible, "with the sword he must be slain."[7] Perhaps the American people will have to learn moral modesty the hard way by becoming the victims of the War on Drugs they now so enthusiastically wage.

State monopoly of the press is a *sine qua non* of a totalitarian society. We regard its opposite, a free press, as one of the pillars on which our open society rests.

Mutatis mutandis, state monopoly of the pharmacopoeia — that is, producing, approving/disapproving, and selling drugs — ought to be considered one of the pillars on which a totalitarian society rests. Yet, we now regard it as a *sine qua non* of our supposedly free society.

Why do we look to science rather than literature for an

understanding of our drug problem? Because science has replaced religion as the socially accredited method for burying our collective head in the sand. In *Erewhon* – a hundred years before the outbreak of the War on Drugs – Samuel Butler offered this explanation of it: "No matter how many laws they [the Erewhonians] passed increasing the severity of punishments inflicted on those who ate meat in secret, the people found means of setting them aside as fast as they were made. . . . [and] when they were on the point of being repealed some national disaster or the preaching of some fanatic would reawaken the conscience of the nation, and people were imprisoned by the thousands for illicitly selling and buying animal food."[8]

Voltaire is supposed to have said: 'I disapprove of what you say, but I will defend to the death your right to say it.'[9] But who will say today: 'I disapprove of what drug you take, but I will defend to the death your right to take it?' Yet it seems to me that the right to take things is more elementary than the right to say things; for taking things is less likely to harm others than saying them. In a free society, it is none of the government's business what idea a man puts into his head; it should also be none of its business what drug he puts into his body.

Isn't it ironic that the United States, the nation that once led the world in preaching and practicing religious tolerance via religious non-interference by the State, now leads the world in preaching and practicing pharmaceutical intolerance via pharmaceutical interference by the State? Much as the Iranians and other God-intoxicated people consider their religious wars sacred – we, (anti) Drug-intoxicated Americans, consider our War on Drugs sacred. But is religious peace not preferable to religious war — letting each person decide which God, if any, to worship? Is pharmacological peace not preferable to pharmacological war — letting each person decide what drug, if any, to ingest, inhale, or inject?

Virtually any activity or substance may be used improperly and may, loosely speaking, 'cause' illegal behavior. For example, religion may influence a person to have more than one wife; literature, to engage in forbidden forms of sexual or political activity. Nevertheless, American law prohibits no creed or book — only behavior, even if it is (allegedly) caused by a 'dangerous' creed or book. We cannot have it any other way with drugs as well: that is, the law can, and should, prohibit illegal behavior, but not illegal drugs. Prohibiting drugs is destined to lead either to widespread defiance of the law and its disastrous concomitants; or, worse still, to the inexorable erosion of our basic legal and political guarantees of individual freedom and responsibility. In short, we must be satisfied with, and prepared to enforce, sanctions against illegal behavior, and reject sanctions against illegal drugs.

The behavior we now call 'drug abuse' (and punish by means of both criminal and psychiatric sanctions) is simply the result of criminalizing and medicalizing what used to be called 'sin'.

The parable of the Fall may rightly be viewed as the paradigm of a person ingesting what he ought not to ingest.

A devout Jew eating ham or a devout Muslim drinking whiskey are examples of sins, that is, breaking religious rules (offenses against God). Murder and theft are examples of crimes, that is, breaking secular rules (offenses against the community, the State). As human beings, we can make — and unmake — such distinctions. Thus, we can transform sins into crimes, crimes into sins, and both into diseases. Which of these conceptual categorizations — that is, sin, crime, disease, or not any of these (that is, acceptable behavior) — we accept or reject depends almost wholly on how we wish to deal with the person who exhibits the (problematic) behavior.

The legitimacy of the government of the United States rests on the fundamental moral-legal principle that it is *not* in the province of the law to forbid ideas, religion, or membership in a group: this is what we mean by the guarantee of freedom of speech, religion, and association. What *is* in the province of the law to prohibit, and of the State to punish, is illegal behavior — regardless of whether it be inspired ('caused') by what we read, what God we worship, or what company we frequent.

Mutatis mutandis, I submit that it is not in the province of American law to forbid drugs or personal status: that is, neither (dangerous) 'drugs' nor (dangerous) 'mental illness' should be prohibited. However, illegal behavior — regardless of whether it be attributed to ('caused' by) drugs or 'mental illness' — should be prohibited by law, and punished by the State.

In short, the pillar on which a truly free society rests is

the principle that the State imposes sanctions *only* against overt behavior, and *only* for the purpose of protecting the public.

EDUCATION

A teacher should have maximal authority, and minimal power.

American public schools glamorize AIDS education, death education, sex education, and suicide education — instead of educating children by demanding that they learn to read, write, and do arithmetic. The result is what one would expect.

According to drug abuse authorities, approximately 10 percent of American physicians abuse drugs. Surely, physicians receive enough education to enable them to comprehend the actions of drugs. If by *education* we mean the imparting of accurate information, then it is clear — from this and other similar examples — that a person may use information to help or harm himself or others, to obey or disobey custom and law.

Information is not — and cannot be — a substitute for self-discipline. 'Drug education', 'sex education', 'suicide education', and other such contemporary slogans are symbols of our unrelenting effort to bury our heads in the sand.

So long as we encourage people, young and old, to believe that the State and Science—with their seemingly limitless financial resources and technical powers—have no more important function than to rescue them from the consequences of their own undisciplined behavior, we in fact teach people to behave in exactly the ways we supposedly don't want them to behave

ETHICS

A glossary:

Bad: Obsolete; superseded by insane, mentally ill, sick.

Good: Obsolete; superseded by sane, mentally healthy, healthy

Ethics: Obsolete; superseded by the diagnosis and treatment of disease.

The liberal-scientific ethic: if it's bad for you, it should be prohibited; if it's good for you, it should be required.

The therapeutic ethic: convict and punish the innocent, and call it mental hospitalization; diagnose and excuse the guilty, and call it the insanity defense.

The safest sin: envy, which is easily disguised as enthusiasm for equality.

The most dangerous virtue: tolerance, which is easily construed as sympathy for subversion.

The principle of tyranny: anyone not for me is against me. The principle of tolerance: anyone not against me is for me.

The three principal rules of conduct:

1. The Golden Rule: Do unto others as you want them to do unto you.

2. The Rule of Respect: Do unto others as they want you to do unto them.

3. The Rule of Paternalism: Do unto others as you, in your superior wisdom, know ought to be done unto them in their own best interests.

Rules of conduct according to the ethics of autonomy:

Criticize the oppressor, but do not humiliate him.

Defend the oppressed, but do not glamorize him.

Respect everyone, regardless of merit or position.

Bestow admiration and love because it is deserved, not because you need others to protect and love you.

Know your enemies; avoid them, if you can; intimidate them if you can't; subdue them, if you must.

Honor your friends; be loyal to them, if you can; warn them, if you can't.

"Nobody may compel me to be happy in his own way," said Kant. "Paternalism is the greatest despotism imaginable."[1] I agree. But it is difficult to imagine what the world would be like if the majority of people believed this and acted accordingly.

To forgive all is to demand all.

"Property is theft," declared Proudhon. This maxim became the credo of the communists and prompted Shaw to declare it "the only perfect truism that has been uttered on the subject."[2]

But suppose a man goes into the mountains, brings back a piece of marble, and carves a beautiful statue out of it. He will have created property: he will 'own' the statue and there will be others who will desire it for themselves. From whom has he stolen it? Truly, the anticapitalist mentality is no less fanatical in its disregard of facts than the revealed religions have been.

When is a choice not a choice? Whenever someone claims it is not and someone else believes him. For example, the agent himself may assert that his choice was not a choice—say, when a man who has killed another claims that he is not guilty of murder by reason of insanity; or someone other than the actor may assert that the actor's choice was not a choice—say, when the parents of a woman who starves herself claim that she is suffering from anorexia nervosa.

Every benefactor wants to control his beneficiary. The priest controls in the name of God; the physician, in the name of health. This universal propensity to control others conflicts with and contradicts the aim of making man a genuine moral agent.

Adam Smith asserted, in effect, that it is more important that the consequences of a person's action be beneficial than that his motives be benevolent. Having good intentions is thus a claim especially fitting for paving contractors bidding on resurfacing hell; persons who parade such a claim are *eo ipso* unfit to guide individuals or groups through the labyrinth of life.

The maxim 'Honesty is the best policy' is incomplete. Completed, it would read: 'Honesty is the best policy toward those who are honest, and the worst toward those who are dishonest.'

Saliva is a watery mucoid secretion in the mouth; spittle is the same thing spit out. This simple distinction epitomizes the basis of most ethical judgements: What is *inside* is ours and is good: what is *outside* is not ours and is bad.

The three justifications for medical (psychiatric) intervention: pathology, permission, paternalism. In other words, treatment may be premised on illness, consent, or (benevolent) coercion.

There is enough infection and death in the world; under no circumstances should the physician himself infect and thus kill his patients. To Ignaz Semmelweis, that seemed like elementary obstetrical ethics.

Mutatis mutandis: There is enough coercion and unfreedom in the world; under no circumstances should the physician (psychiatrist) himself coerce and thus render (even more) unfree his patients. To me, this seems like elementary psychiatric ethics.

If a person claims that a 'compulsion' causes him to conduct himself in a way he does not want to, then it becomes reasonable to 'compel' him by force to submit to 'treatment' to enable him to resist his involuntary behavior. Thus have compulsion and compulsory treatment displaced responsibility and punishment.

In our age, Liberalism (statism) and psychiatry have conspired not so much to destroy the concept of responsibility as to pervert it. I refer to the ethical outlook — widely accepted by contemporary intellectuals and progressives as scientific — that human failure is due to inadequate parents or social systems, but that human achievement is the result of creativity, intelligence, and hard work: we are not responsible for our bad deeds and should not be punished for them, but we are responsible for our good deeds and should be praised and rewarded for them.

The psychiatrization of ethics cuts both ways, one more familiar than the other. One is to use psychiatric explanations to make bad behavior (one's own or that of others) look good or at least not blameworthy, as in the insanity defense. The other is to use psychiatric explanations to make good behavior look bad or at least not praiseworthy, in what might be called the 'insanity offense': for example, a person might attribute his own loyalty and reliability to guilt or the desire to avoid disapproval or a zealous anti-capitalist might attribute the affluence and peacefulness of the Swiss to greed and cowardliness. In all these manifestations we see psychiatry at work — undermining, confusing, and destroying our sense of right and wrong.

"It does seem" — laments Barbara Tuchman — "that the knowledge of the difference between right and wrong is absent from our society, as if it had floated away on a shadowy night after the last World War. So remote is the concept that even to speak of right and wrong marks one to the younger generation as old-fashioned, reactionary, and out of touch."[3]

Ironically, Tuchman herself has been an enthusiastic supporter of the mental health movement and a prominent practitioner of the art of psychohistory, enterprises whose main mission has been the very destruction of the differences between right and wrong that she bewails. More than a quarter of a century ago, I warned against this danger,[4] citing the program for modern psychiatry outlined by Brock Chisholm at the end of World War II: "The reinterpretation and eventual eradication of the concept of right and wrong . . . are the belated objectives of all effective psychotherapy. . . . If the race is to be freed from its crippling burden of good and evil, it must be the psychiatrists who take the original responsibility. This is a challenge which must be met."[5]

Psychiatrists have met the challenge and, aided and abetted by intellectuals, journalists, clergymen, and jurists, helped to destroy the difference between right and wrong and replace it with the difference between mentally healthy and mentally ill.

In the United States today, the legal penalty for killing another person with poison may be less than it is for 'poisoning' oneself with certain prohibited drugs. Nothing could more dramatically symbolize that we now regard heteronomy as blessed and autonomy as cursed.

A gun is fired and as a result a person suffers a bullet wound. Such a person is *injured*. He is *sick*. He is a *patient*.

For most people today, the last three sentences assert the same proposition, namely, that such a person has a disease — a bullet wound. Insofar as people now believe (as many do) that it is irrelevant or even immoral to inquire into the details of such a 'patient's' personal and social situation; that all such 'patients' are victims who have a right to medical care (and perhaps to much more); in short, to the extent to which their gaze encompasses only objects, such as guns, bullets, and wounds, and excludes persons as moral agents — to that extent we have lost the ability to make the morally relevant discriminations and judgments necessary at every moment of our waking life. Physicians are not exempt from this rule: Possessing medical credentials ought to increase, rather than diminish, this universal moral burden of being human.

Although we extol individual liberty and responsibility, we have not yet reached the stage of truly valuing autonomy: In the past, the ideal person was one who allowed himself to be *saved* by God or Jesus — in short, by divine intervention; today, the ideal person is one who allows himself to be *treated* by medical Science or physicians — in short, by medical intervention.

Every creed, philosophy, political system that prescribes how people should live is bound to be wrong — in the sense that it sets itself against the fundamental human needs for autonomy and diversity.

Like space, time is a kind of territory. As contending armies cannot occupy the same geographic territory, so contending activities cannot occupy the same time. Should man spend his time worshipping God, procreating and nurturing future generations, or creating objects or spectacles that amuse or please others?

Oriental man, devoid of a tradition of capitalism and individual liberty, sees meditation as the broadest and most beautiful boulevard leading to (what he calls) enlightenment. Occidental man, bolstered by a tradition of capitalism and individual liberty, sees work useful for others as the broadest and most beautiful boulevard leading to (what he calls) prosperity and a higher standard of living. Since each tradition reinforces its own moral premises and neither can accommodate the other, it is small wonder that when East and West meet, each thinks the other has found The Way.

To survive as organisms, we must destroy other living things (animals, vegetables) and live off the chemicals of which they are composed as physical objects; in this sense, we are 'biological cannibals'. Similarly, to survive as social beings, we must invalidate other human beings (scapegoats) and live off the legitimacy of which they are composed as spiritual beings. This is what I mean when I say that we are—indeed, seem condemned to be—'existential cannibals'. Only after recognizing this can we intelligently consider which form of existential cannibalism is morally superior or inferior to which other and why.

In the eternal struggle between good and evil, good is at an irreducible disadvantage: it has no future—whereas evil does. Since human beings are fundamentally future-oriented, they have an insatiable incentive for being fascinated with evil in all its guises — that is, with guilt and shame, poverty and stupidity, crime, sin, and madness. Each of these is susceptible, at least in principle, to being reformed, remedied, or righted in one way or another. But what can a person do with what is good — except admire it? Good thus frustrates precisely that 'therapeutic' ambition in the human soul which evil satisfies so perfectly. Hence, Voltaire should also have said that if there were no devil, we would have to invent him.

INSANITY DEFENSE

Insanity defense: 1. Formerly, a tactic for classifying/legitimizing the defendant as the type of malefactor upon whom the state cannot (legitimately) impose a death penalty. 2. Today, a tactic for classifying/legitimizing the defendant as the type of malefactor whose management should be diverted from the criminal justice system to the mental health system. 3. One of the sacred rituals of psychiatry, often confused—especially by the public, the press, and psychiatrists—with the scientific search, by a lay jury, in a court of law, for the ultimate causes of human (mis)behavior.

The insanity defense and the insanity verdict are joined in holy matrimony in the insanity trial: The defendant claims the nonexistent condition of insanity as an excuse for what he did to his victim: the court claims the same nonexistent condition as a justification for what it does to the defendant.

Formerly, Americans charged with murder were considered innocent until proven guilty; now they are considered insane until proven sane.

People, especially liberals and psychiatrists, say that the two main causes of crime are mental illness and poverty. Insanity is therefore a defense in the criminal law. If we really believed that poverty caused crime, we would have a 'poverty defense' as well, attorneys calling professors of economics to testify in court whether a particular defendant is guilty of theft or not guilty by reason of poverty.

Obesity is the name we give to the bodily condition of being overweight. When a person overeats, he becomes, or we say he is, obese. Accordingly, it would be absurd to say that obesity *causes* overeating.

Mutatis mutandis, schizophrenia is the name we give to the mental condition of engaging in certain prohibited behaviors (for example, shooting a stranger for 'no reason'). When a person behaves in such a way, he becomes, or we say he is, schizophrenic. Accordingly, it is absurd to say that schizophrenia *causes* a person to behave in a certain abnormal way (and hence excuses such behavior).

Gastroenterologists cannot ascertain what was in

another person's stomach days, weeks, or months ago; but psychiatrists can certify what was in his mind days, weeks, months, or even years ago.

   The popular belief that "society is responsible for crime, and criminals are not responsible for crime," Arnold W. Green points out, amounts to the view "that only those members of society who do not commit a crime can be held responsible for crime. Nonsense this obvious can be circumvented only by conjuring up society as devil, as evil apart from people and what they do."[1] Insanity as evil apart from what a specific (ostensibly) insane individual does is perhaps an even more obvious nonsense; but even more appealing because it makes an illness rather than society the culprit.

   Legally punishing and psychiatrically understanding persons who break the law are two mutually incompatible enterprises. Jacques Barzun has said all there is to say about this, but few people have listened: " . . . the advocacy of various brands of 'cure' for crime in effect cripple the law. For with the usual futurism of science, the new intention is held justified by its goodwill alone: the newspapers are full of assaults and murders committed by 'cured' mental patients . . . everywhere the application of a crude social and psychological causality is undermining the power of the social compact and the responsibility of the individual."[2]

The idea that a person is responsible for his criminal act regardless of who ordered him to break the law is now widely accepted in relation to political crimes, but not in relation to domestic crimes. But why should we treat deceiving Congress differently than destroying one's wife or husband? Declared the prosecutor in the trial of Oliver North:

> When an individual is asked a question by Congress, there are only two legitimate responses: the individual may decline to answer the question, or answer it honestly. He cannot with impunity . . . answer with a falsehood. . . . [North's] alleged motivation for lying is irrelevant to the charges against him.[3]

Mutatis mutandis, I maintain that a person who believes he should kill someone has only two choices: he must control himself and not do so, or he must kill himself. The defendant's alleged motivation for the murder—say, the claim that God commanded him to kill—should be irrelevant to the charge against him.

It is self-evident that the so-called mentally ill criminal has committed a crime. What psychiatrists contend, and what most people now accept, is not that 'insane criminals' do not commit crimes, but only that they do so from psychotic motives, exemplified by the phrase 'I heard God's voice and he told me to kill my child.' But "Crimes," asserted Sir Hartley Shawcross at the Nuremberg trials of the Nazi war criminals, "do not cease to be criminal because they have a political motive."[4] By the same token, I maintain that crimes do not cease to be criminal because they have a 'psychotic' motive.

A French proverb admonishes: '*Qui s'éxcuse, s'accusé*' ('He who excuses himself, accuses himself.') Similarly, he whom we excuse, we also accuse. This explains why the entire edifice of psychiatry rests so heavily on the insanity defense, which formally recognizes psychiatrists as legitimate excusers (and accusers). It is the tragedy of the modern mental-patient liberation movements, and a testimony to the 'normal' selfishness of their members, that while former mental patients indignantly condemn psychiatric accusations justifying involuntary mental hospitalization, they stubbornly refuse to condemn psychiatric excuses justifying the insanity defense.

LANGUAGE

Medical mendacities:

The prevention of parenthood — called "planned parenthood."

Homicide by physicians — called "euthanasia."

Imprisonment by psychiatrists — called "mental hospitalization."

Words as pretexts:

Delusion: A pretext for incarcerating troublesome persons (and calling it 'mental hospitalization').

Anti-psychotic medication: A pretext for evicting persons from mental hospitals (and calling it 'deinstitutionalization').

Insanity defense: A pretext for depriving people of responsibility and liberty (and calling it 'non-responsibility due to mental illness').

Quod licet Jovi, non licet bovi (What is permitted to Jove, is not permitted to the cow):

Policemen receive bribes; politicians, campaign contributions.

General Motors advertises automobiles; the American Psychiatric Association educates about mental illness.

Marijuana is sold by pushers; tobacco, by merchants.

The patient who goes to court to get out of the mental hospital is paranoid; the psychiatrist who goes to court to get him into the mental hospital is therapeutic.

When the patient fakes illness, he 'malingers'; when the healer fakes treatment, he prescribes a 'placebo' or practices 'psychotherapy'.

Ingesting a prohibited drug is called 'drug abuse'; ingesting a prescribed drug is called 'chemotherapy'.

The mental patient's explanations of his experiences are called 'delusions' and 'fantasies'; the psychiatrist's explanations of them are called 'diagnoses' and 'interpretations'.

A person may use force to compel another person to work — we call that 'slavery'; or to change his religion — we call that 'coerced religious conversion'; or to submit to a sexual act — we call that 'rape'. However, if a person uses force to compel another person to be incarcerated in a psychiatric institution, we call it 'hospitalization'; and if he uses force to compel another person to ingest a psychiatric drug, we call it 'treatment'.

In hospital psychiatry, the best way to tell the patient from the psychiatrist is by who has the keys; in nonhospital psychiatry, by who has the key words.

Ideologue: A person who uses ideas as incantations. True believer: A person who accepts incantations as ideas. Skeptic: A person who assumes that ideas are incantations until proven otherwise.

Aphorism is to description as caricature is to portrait.

In the animal kingdom, the rule is: eat or be eaten; in the human kingdom: define or be defined.

Language separates men from other animals. It also reduces them to the level of animals — as in calling Jews 'vermin' or policemen 'pigs'.

It is likely that aboriginal man first vocalized idiosyncratically, each man making noise rather than speaking a

language. When two or more individuals adapted their
noisemaking to a common pattern, language was born.
Language may thus constitute the original social contract,
out of which grew all the others.

Analogy is a conceptual instrument constructed by
means of the proper arrangement of words, much as the
microscope and the telescope are optical instruments constructed by means of the proper arrangement of lenses. If
an object is too small or too far to be perceptible with the
naked eye, we may be able to see it by viewing it through
an optical instrument. Similarly, if an idea is emotionally
too close or too far for us to perceive it, we may be able to
see it by viewing it through an analogy.

Metaphor is a verbal cartoon. Hence, it must be
grasped, not analyzed.

"The greatest thing by far," says Aristotle, "is to be a
master of metaphor. It is the one thing that cannot be learnt
from others."[1] The human fear of freedom and love of
dependence is perhaps nowhere displayed more tragically
than in the one-sided application of this profound truth.
Persons who create new metaphors and use them literally
to enslave others—for example, Marx and Freud—are acclaimed as great liberators; whereas those who unravel the
literalized metaphors of oppressors and thus liberate others

—for example, Karl Kraus and Henry Mencken—are belittled as destructive cynics.

Mathematics is a language without metaphors. That is why it is the perfect tool for conveying precise meaning—and perfectly useless for inspiring people.

Music is a language with nothing but metaphors. That is why it is the perfect tool for moving people (as in religious or martial music)—and why it is perfectly useless for conveying any precise meaning whatever.

Religion and the jargon of the helping/hindering professions are comprised largely of literalized metaphors. That is why they are the perfect tools for legitimizing and illegitimizing ideas, behaviors, and persons.

Ordinary language combines all of these qualities. It can be used literally and precisely, to convey meaning; metaphorically or poetically, to move people; or 'religiously', to blind and numb people, making them feel elevated or debased.

Bracketed as art, metaphor is poetry; bracketed as witticism, humor; bracketed as worship, religion; and bracketed as insanity, illness.

Adam's apple is so named because a piece of the Biblical forbidden fruit is supposed to have stuck in his throat. The name *Adam* itself is the Hebrew word for 'man'. What sticks in our throat, then, is the Truth — specifically, the Forbidden Truth. When we manage to cough up the bolus and inspect it, what do we see? Not any kind of fruit (apple is not mentioned in the Bible), but a masticated mass of some not easily identifiable substance. Perhaps this is why the Forbidden Truth so often appears 'chewed up', transformed into metaphor, humor, satire, slang (or dream and myth, of course).

Lord Palmerston wisely cautioned that "Half the wrong conclusions at which mankind arrive are reached by the abuse of metaphors."[2] True. But how do we know — who decides — whether a metaphor is used or abused? Is it used or abused in the Bible? In the story of the origin of the Ten Commandments? In the doctrine of transubstantiation? In the libido theory?

Again and again we come back to the realization that if controlling man is the destination, the road to it lies through control of language.

A person who feels sad may be said to be dejected or depressed. A person who claims to be God, may be said to be boasting or deluded. The difference between these descriptions is the same as the difference between calling a spade a shovel or an agricultural implement for soil penetration — or between calling a man 'a black' or 'a nigger'.

When I explain, at a person's own request, why I say that deviant behaviors (like gambling or claiming to be God) are not diseases (like cancer or diabetes), and my interlocutor says: 'But that's *only* semantics', then I know I am not answering his question because he hasn't asked me a question.

From the admission note in a psychiatric hospital record: "Patient has not been auditorily hallucinated." This phrase exemplifies the transformation of an individual from subject to object — from a moral agent who experiences his being in the world and reports on it, to a thing upon which natural events impinge, like rain falling on a rooftop. It is precisely this transformation which promotes and perpetuates the relentless victimization of psychiatric patients by psychiatric doctors through the guise of psychiatric diagnoses and treatments.

Students of language have aptly noted that the man on-the-street does not know that he talks in prose. Might we not say, in the same way, that the ordinary mental patient does not know that he talks in metaphor? And that the psychiatrist and the intelligent layman also don't realize it?

The Greeks distinguished between good and bad behavior, language that enhanced or diminished persons. Being intoxicated with scientism, we fail to recognize that the seemingly technical terms used to identify psychiatric illnesses and interventions are simply dysphemisms and euphemisms.

In the natural sciences, language (mathematics) is a useful tool: like the microscope or telescope, it enables us to see what is otherwise invisible. In the social sciences, language (literalized metaphors) is an impediment: like a distorting mirror, it prevents us from seeing the obvious.

That is why in the natural sciences, knowledge can be gained only with the mastery of their special languages; whereas in human affairs, knowledge can be gained only by rejecting the pretentious jargons of the social sciences.

Atheists are often called 'anti-religious', but religious persons are never called 'anti-atheists'. The fact that ordinary language is not — indeed, cannot be — neutral toward important human affairs must be recognized as one of its most important features.

We now use the metaphor of alcohol addiction with great abandon — speaking, for example, of workaholics, spendaholics, chocaholics, foodaholics, and so forth. But never do we speak of Godaholics or moneyholics.

Definers (persons who insist on defining others) are like pathogenic micro-organisms: both invade, parasitize, and often destroy their victims. As persons with poor immunological defenses are most likely to contract infectious diseases, so persons with poor social defenses — the young and the old, the sick and the poor — are most likely to contract invidious definitions of themselves.

"He who excuses himself, accuses himself," says a French proverb. In other words, the person who speaks in the language of excuses — advancing disability, illness, mental illness, ignorance, or poverty as an excuse — has lost half the battle for self-esteem before he has begun to fight it.

The rhetoricians of race are not content with repudiating the oppression of the Negro, but claim that 'black is beautiful'; the rhetoricians of drugs are not content with rejecting false claims about the harmfulness of certain drugs, but assert that toxic chemicals 'expand the mind'; the rhetoricians of madness are not content with opposing psychiatric fraud and force, but claim that schizophrenia is 'not a breakdown but a breakthrough'. In short, ours is an age in which partial truths are tirelessly transformed into

total falsehoods and then acclaimed as revolutionary
revelations.

George Orwell foresaw Big Brother controlling us by
means of a 'thought police'. Perhaps he should have called
them 'language police', since it is only language, not
thought, that can be policed. Indeed, language has been
policed in the past, in the name of religion, and is policed
now, in the name of human rights. For example, Jesse
Jackson has declared that the term 'blacks' is out: "Just as we
were called colored but were not that, and then Negro, but
not that, to be called black is just as baseless. To be called
African-American has cultural integrity. . . . the title or
name African-American points us to a higher consciousness
in terms of the origin of African peoples." Mr. Jackson, the
New York Times reported, "said he would start using the
term immediately."[3]

"Words that are saturated with lies or atrocity," writes
George Steiner, "do not easily resume life."[4] This is why the
languages of both madness and mad-doctoring are dead
languages. The speaker of each tries to deny his own mendacity: the madman, through the fraudulent rhetoric of his
'symptoms'; the mad doctor, through the fraudulent
rhetoric of his 'diagnoses' and 'treatments'.

Sartre, too, remarks on the role of the lie in the
language of psychoanalysis. "Psychoanalysis," he writes,
"substitutes for the notion of bad faith the idea of a lie
without a liar; . . . it replaces the duality of the deceiver and
the deceived, the essential condition of the lie, by that of

the 'id' and the 'ego'."[5] But by rehabilitating the lie, psycho-analysis annihilates the truth.

As the swimmer depends on water, so the writer depends on language. To swim well, we must let ourselves be enveloped by the water, sink into it, become a part of it. To write well, we must similarly let ourselves be enveloped by the language, sink into it, become a part of it. In short, as swimmers, instead of fighting the water to avoid drowning, we must learn to use our body-in-the-water so it will float effortlessly: then, we can start to swim. Similarly, as writers, instead of fighting the language to make it express our ideas, we must learn to use our mind-in-the-language so that our ideas-in-words will float effortlessly: then, we can start to write.

For the Jew, God is Lord, not lord; and a Lord cannot have a son, only a lord can. For the Christian, God is both Lord and lord; hence, He can have a son who, himself, is both man and God, lord and Lord. The Jewish idea of God is pure metaphor, whereas the Christian idea of it is a combination of metaphor and literalized metaphor.

We have two kinds of screwdrivers: one for turning screws, another for drinking. We also have two kinds of patients: one for treating medically, another for coercing psychiatrically.

'Homosexuality' is the name we give to the preference for sexual intercourse with members of one's own sex. Would calling preference for marriage with members of one's own race and religion 'homoraciality' and 'homoreligiosity' make them mental diseases? Would the members of the American Psychiatric Association vote on whether or not they are mental diseases?

Had the white settlers in North America called the natives 'Americans' instead of 'Indians', the early Americans could not have said that 'The only good Indian is a dead Indian' and could not have deprived them so easily of their lands and lives. Robbing people of their proper names is often the first step in robbing them of their property, liberty, and life.

When the Swiss are for nonintervention in war, they are called 'neutral'; when Americans are for nonintervention, they are called 'isolationists'.

Discussing psychiatric problems at international conferences with persons whose English is imperfect is like dueling with someone who grabs his sword by the blade: one is inhibited from pressing an intellectual argument on an interlocutor wounded by his very handling of the instrument of our communication.

Physicians and mental health professionals are fond of referring to nearly everyone as a 'patient'—a linguistic habit that has gone largely unnoticed and unchallenged. But the change, especially if involuntary, from person to patient is similar to that from citizen to subject, even freeman to slave. Politicians would not endure if they referred to people indiscriminately as their subjects or slaves; neither should physicians who refer to people indiscriminately as their patients.

Clear speech and writing betoken sincerity and respect for the rules of language, thus implying a willingness to eschew coercion by communication. Since the human larynx and tongue may easily be used as claws and fangs—and words as venom—it is easy to understand why the unilateral verbal disarmament of semantic pacifism is both feared and admired.

Our body is composed of what we eat; our mind, of what we hear, read, say, and write. This is why every society, every social institution—religion, law, medicine—controls not only what we can and cannot take into our bodies, but also what we can and cannot take into our minds. In the final analysis, control of food is tantamount to control of the body, and control of language to control of the mind.

All writing betokens conceit—that one has something

worthwhile to say. Writing philosophy betokens intellectual conceit—that one has something fresh to say about the
human condition; writing poetry, emotional conceit—that
one has sensitivities and sentiments worth sharing with
strangers; and writing aphorisms, esthetic conceit—that
one can say something worthwhile elegantly and entertain-
ingly.

As organisms (bodies) we live in physical space; as persons (minds), in linguistic space. This is why a country is a
matter of geography, but a nation a matter of language.

To survive as organisms, animals need physical territory—and they struggle for it. As organisms, we too are
animals—and struggle for such territory. However, to survive as spiritual beings or persons, we need a secure and
legitimate mental rather than physical turf. Our spiritual
territoriality is displayed in the unceasing effort to make
others share our religious fictions and adopt our linguistic
conventions—in short, to worship our God, speak our
language, and be like-minded persons.

We *use* things, but we *relate* to persons. Since we do
not—and must not!—use persons, we cannot properly
speak of abusing them. Instead, we ought to speak of
relating to them lovingly or hatefully, honestly or
dishonestly, forgivingly or revengefully, and so forth. Our
fondness for phrases such as 'child abuse', 'wife abuse',
'elder abuse', reveals how profoundly disrespectful we are

toward the personhood of children and other powerless persons whose best interests we allegedly seek to protect.

Infants, idiots, and the insane *need* things; normal adults *want* things. The language of needs is the native tongue of socialists, therapeutists, and paternalists of all sorts and is addressed to needy dependents; whereas the language of wants is spoken by self-respecting persons (adults) and is addressed to other self-respecting persons.

Verbal intercourse is a form of intimacy, often more intense than sexual intercourse. Actually, conversation is more indispensable for personal survival than copulation. This is why religions that cultivate other-worldliness (especially Christianity) extoll, as a cardinal virtue, not only celibacy but also silence. Revealingly, the English word *parlor*—from the French, *parler*, 'to talk'—referred originally to a room in a monastery or nunnery where conversations were permitted, in particular between members of the religious order and visitors from the outside world.

Modern medicalized psychiatry denies the quintessential intimacy of verbal intercourse. Hence the debauchery of referring to psychotherapy as something a doctor *gives* a patient, as though it were an enterprise in which any two persons could promiscuously engage. I say "promiscuously" because such a view implies that people can converse with one another regardless of who they are or what they value.

Masturbation — that is, satisfying the sexual urge alone, by and for oneself — was long considered to be both the cause and consequence of the severest forms of insanity (a belief that persisted well into the first half of this century). Verbal masturbation — that is, satisfying the urge for semantic intimacy alone, by and for oneself — is still so regarded.

Psychiatrists as well as lay persons firmly believe that 'hearing voices' is the manifestation of a malignant mental disease and that this mental symptom is itself so dangerous to mental health that it ought to be suppressed by whatever means necessary — such as lobotomy, electroshock, or neuroleptic drugs.

It took medical science and public opinion the better part of two hundred years to realize and recognize that sexual self-satisfaction was not an illness and did not cause illness. Perhaps it will take even longer for medical science and public opinion to realize and recognize that semantic self-satisfaction is similarly neither a symptom of disease nor a justification for (involuntary) treatment.

Men are rewarded or punished not for what they do, but for how their acts are defined. That is why men are more interested in better justifying themselves than in better behaving themselves.

In the Greco-Roman world in which the Jews of antiquity lived people were obsessed with deities and religion. The Greeks had many gods and goddesses. So did the Romans. But the Jews had only one. Dissatisfied with monotheism, some Jews must have wanted to have more gods or at least one other — more visible and real than their invisible and unnameable deity: So they invented Jesus, the Son of God — an easy literalization of the then common metaphoric phrase, 'son of God'.

We moderns, obsessed with disease and treatment, do the same: Dissatisfied with the strict (mono-criterial) conception of disease as bodily abnormality, we invent new diseases more susceptible to manipulation by the will (our own or that of another with the power to coerce) than are real diseases: So we invent smoking, drinking, and other (bad) habits as diseases — easy literalizations of the now common metaphoric phrase, 'it's a sickness'.

LAW

The state cannot 'legalize' an act; it can only prohibit it by law, or leave it alone.

Traditional justice is based on the concepts of right and wrong; modern justice, on mental health and illness. Faced with two women both of whom claimed to be the mother of the same child, Solomon talked to them, listened to them, and awarded the child to the woman who, he inferred from the information he obtained, was the real mother. A modern American judge would proceed quite differently. Faced with two such women, he would conclude that one of them must be deluded. Then, he would order both to be examined by psychiatrists, who would duly discover that one of the women is a fanatic, insisting that she wants the whole child or nothing, whereas the other is reasonable, willing to compromise and accept half a child. Accordingly, the psychiatrist would declare the real mother to be suffering from schizophrenia, and recommend awarding the child to the imposter—a recommendation the judge, respectful of the findings of medical experts, would rubber-stamp.

An old proverb cautions the would-be lawmaker not to

prohibit what he cannot enforce. Modern American law-makers follow the opposite rule; they are most zealous to prohibit that which they cannot enforce.

If the person who breaks the law is not punished, the person who obeys it is cheated. This is why lawbreakers ought to be punished: to encourage law-abiding behavior as useful and to authenticate it as virtuous. The aim of the criminal law cannot and must not be correction; it can only be, and must be, the maintenance of the legal order.

Punishment is now unfashionable. Why? Because it creates moral distinctions among men, which, to the democratic mind, are odious. We prefer a meaningless collective guilt to a meaningful individual responsibility.

There can be no humane penology so long as punishment masquerades as correction. No person or group has the right to correct another adult: only God does. But persons and groups have the right to protect themselves by means of punishments, which may be as mild as a scolding or a small fine, or as harsh as life imprisonment or death.

Biological psychiatrists claim that mental diseases are caused by, or are the manifestations of, underlying bodily diseases — as yet undiscovered but waiting to be discovered by progress in medical science. If this proved to be true for some or all mental diseases, it would only add more items to the existing list of organic diseases whose treatment patients are free to reject. Hence, evidence supporting the organic etiology of so-called mental illness would display rather than dispel the moral and political dilemmas of coercive psychiatry.

Clarence Darrow is supposed to have said that he was for divorce because he was against murder. It is indeed better that husband and wife divorce than commit violence against each other. Similarly, wouldn't it be better for psychiatrist and mental patient to divorce instead of commit violence against each other? In other words, instead of the psychiatrist being allowed to injure the patient with commitment, and the patient the psychiatrist with litigation for false imprisonment, each would be allowed to sever his relationship with the other. Such an arrangement would preclude the psychiatrist's violating the patient with what the psychiatrist calls 'treatment', but the patient experiences as assault; and the patient's violating the psychiatrist with what the patient calls 'self-defense', but the psychiatrist experiences as assault.

I contend that psychiatric incarceration is always and necessarily a violation of human rights. Why? Because the psychiatric jailer, unlike the penological jailer, claims to be, and may sincerely believe himself to be, a legitimate double agent — protecting the patient from himself (or from mental illness), and society from the patient. Insofar as the psychiatrist is accepted as serving the patient's interests, the patient is deprived of legitimizing his grievance against the psychiatrist's treatment; insofar as the psychiatrist is accepted as serving society's interests, the psychiatrist is protected from legitimate criticism for depriving the patient of his liberty.

A court of law can be one thing only: an organ for legitimizing coercion. It cannot be what activist judges and their sympathizers want it to be: an organ of benevolence or social justice. Hence it is that court-ordered remedies for social ills, such as mandating treatment for involuntarily hospitalized mental patients, cannot solve, but can only aggravate, the problems they ostensibly seek to ameliorate.

The very act of speaking of protecting the 'civil rights of mental patients' is an injury to their civil rights. For just as speaking of the 'civil rights of slaves' implicitly legitimizes the legal distinction between slaves and free men and hence deprives the former of liberties and dignities enjoyed by the latter, so speaking of the 'civil rights of mental patients' implicitly legitimizes the legal distinction between insane patients and sane citizens and hence deprives the former of liberties and dignities enjoyed by the latter.

Not until a free people accept and demand that civil rights be independent of psychiatric criteria, just as they now are of religious criteria—and not until legislators and jurists deprive physicians, and especially psychiatrists, of the power to exercise social controls by means of quasi-medical sanctions — will the civil rights of persons accused of mental illness be protected.

For years, American health authorities have been promoting the use of condoms as a means of practicing 'safe sex' to prevent both AIDS and unwanted pregnancy. Yet many local ordinances in the United States (for example, in Syracuse, New York) continue to prohibit the sale of condoms through vending machines or from anyone other than a licensed physician or pharmacist. Violators could be fined $150 and imprisoned for up to 150 days.[1] The law is not enforced, of course.

Legitimacy

Sources of legitimacy:

God (Religion, the Church, the Pope)

The Sovereign (Emperor, King, Monarch)

The State (Parliament, the Law, the People)

Tradition (Custom, 'When in Rome do as the Romans do')

Paternalism (Family, Parent, Expert)

Dependency (Need, Illness, Poverty)

Reason (Science, Medicine, Health)

The Self (Individual rights, Autonomy)

What legitimizes one person's getting what he wants from another?

In family relations and in Christianity: dependency and need. Infants have a 'right' to get protection and support from their parents; the poor and the clergy have a 'right' to get protection and support from the rich. This is why parents must be responsible for their children, and the rich must be responsible for the poor and the clergy.

In war and in despotic-totalitarian countries: power. The victors and the rulers have a 'right' to get from the vanquished and the people what they want. This is why the weak must be submissive toward the strong.

In capitalism: money. Persons with money have a 'right' to get what they want from those willing to give it to them in exchange for money. This is why the free market tends to equalize human relations, making capitalism not only efficient but also ethical.

Formerly, God was our grand legitimizer; today, it's Mental Health. For anyone who doubts it, I offer the following supporting evidence:

> DEAR ABBY: I recently lost my wife . . . At the wake, knowing that after the casket was closed I would not see her again until I joined her in eternity . . . I shed a few tears as I said goodbye and planted a farewell kiss on her cold and silent lips. The clergyman (I am a former clergyman) . . . became highly incensed because of having the viewing in the first place, talking to my wife while she lay in her casket, and kissing her . . . After the viewing, he telephoned me and 'laid me out in lavender' . . . suggesting I was a mental case and in need of a psychiatrist. . . . Abby, . . . what do you think of this minister? BEN FROM BROCKTON.

> DEAR BEN: Forgive your minister . . . I think he is a troubled man and his behavior should be reported to whomever is his superior.[7]

As in the Age of Faith everyone's behavior — especially that of the Prince — was contingent on its being viewed as legitimate because in conformity with God's design, so in the Age of Mental Health everyone's behavior — especially that of the Therapist — is contingent on its being viewed as legitimate because in conformity with criteria of mental health. How else could we account for the fact that "Ben's" minister illegitimizes his parishioner's behavior by pronouncing him "in need of a psychiatrist"? That "Ben", himself a former minister, seeks to restore his legitimacy not by consulting the Bible or Christian tradition or his own conscience (as a Protestant minister in the past might have done), but by submitting his case to the judgment of Dear Abby, a leading authority on Mental Health? And that Dear Abby herself uses the vocabulary of psychobabble to illegitimize the illegitimizer by categorizing him as a [mentally] "troubled man"?

Declaring that one does not like Jones is much weaker than diagnosing him as mentally sick. If we describe our adversary in plain English — as hostile or threatening — we continue to recognize him as fully human; but if we diagnose him in the defamatory rhetoric of psychiatry or antipsychiatry — as mad or mentally ill — than we no longer recognize him as fully human. Herein lies the appeal of the madness-mongering imagery and language of both psychiatry and antipsychiatry: each renders the speaker effortlessly superior to his adversary.

Physicians stubbornly believe that there are two types

of pains, organic and psychogenic. The organic, they insist, is caused by a lesion in the body: the psychogenic, by one in the mind. In fact, physicians do not experience, and cannot properly classify, other people's pains. What they experience and classify are other people's complaints. Complaints of pain which doctors consider legitimate, they validate as 'organic'; those they consider illegitimate, they invalidate as 'psychogenic'.

Hence, it is a mistake to believe that organic pain is one kind of pain, and psychogenic pain another kind, the former standing in the same relation to the latter as, say, ureteral colic stands to biliary colic. Instead, organic pain is a legitimate complaint and psychogenic pain an illegitimate complaint, the one standing in the same relation to the other as, for example, real money stands to fake money or counterfeit.

"Anything," declares sportswriter Wally Hall, "that could sideline a man who had the promise and potential [Bill] Brown did has to be considered a disease."[2] Announcing that something — anything — is a disease has become our favorite indoor sport. Like reflagging Kuwaiti tankers to justify treating them as if they were bona fide American property, we pin the label 'disease' on anything and everything so that we can legitimately think or do whatever we want to think or do in the mindless pursuit of our momentary self-interest.

Language, the oldest and still most reliable guide to a people's true sentiments, starkly reveals the intimate connections among illness, indignity, and illegitimacy. In English, we use the same word to describe an expired passport, an indefensible argument, an illegitimate legal document, and a person disabled by disease: We call each 'invalid'. To be an invalid, then, is to be an invalidated person, a human stamped 'Not Valid' by the invisible but invincible hand of popular opinion. While invalidism carries with it the heaviest burden of indignity and illegitimacy, some stigma adheres to virtually all illness, to virtually any participation in the role of patient.

Inanimate objects and animals exist in physical space and their behavior exhibits regularities which we call physical or biological laws. Human beings, *qua* persons, exist in social space and their behavior exhibits regularities which we ascribe to their obeying (or disobeying) God's laws, Natural law, the Moral law, the laws of Monarchs, Parties, or Electorates, the Principles of Psychology, or the dictates of their own conscience. Being in harmony with the prescriptions and proscriptions of Law — be it God's, the State's, the Medical Profession's, one's own — gives rise to a sense of legitimacy, its absence, to a sense of illegitimacy.

Because we are spiritual-social beings, the human desire for legitimacy may be even more basic than the desire for life itself: Sometimes, some persons want to die; but no one ever wants to be illegitimate. Illegitimacy, *par excellence*, is an ascription no one attributes to himself: Even the person guilty of a grave moral sin or crime — a Judas, a Lady Macbeth, a modern mass murderer — views himself not as an *illegitimate person* but as a *legitimate sinner* or *criminal*.

In short, legitimacy is to us what water is to fish: the

milieu in which we, as spiritual beings, live—and hence notice only when we are deprived of it (by others). Revealingly, when we deprive others of legitimacy, we tend to blind ourselves to the subject's situation as he experiences it: We insist that his situation is caused by *his* condition, not by *our* definition. Indeed, no sooner do we perceive an illegitimate actor's situation as due to our own doing than the negative ascription quickly loses its legitimacy and disappers. The concept of 'illegitimate child' is a case in point: Thought to be tainted by a moral defect of his parents, such a child was believed to be significantly different from a legitimate child. *Mutatis mutandis,* an insane person—thought to be tainted by a chromosomal defect of his parents—is now believed to be significantly different from a sane person.

But if insanity is a type of illegitimacy, the question we must answer is: Is it fair to categorize a person as insane? I believe it is unfair to the so-called patient, when the categorization is used to incriminate him as mentally ill and justify involuntarily confining or treating him; and it is unfair to society, when it is used to exculpate him as not responsible for his actions, publicly support him without expecting socially acceptable behavior from him, and exclude him from the category of persons we regard as morally deserving of punishment.

Because man is a social animal, he must live in a group and secure a measure of cohesion in it. The best and easiest (and perhaps only) way to do so is by means of the dramatic persecution of the Other—as in Crusades, witch hunts, wars on Jews, drugs, and mental illness. Moreover, because man is a moral agent with a sense of right and wrong, he must justify/legitimize his existential cannibalism. The best and easiest (and perhaps only) way to do so is by means of the dual claim that the control/destruction of the Other is necessary: 1. to protect the purity and safety of the group; and 2. to save the soul/mental health of the Other.

How are these rationalizations supported? In the Age of Faith, by belief in immortality and prayer for the Other's soul. In the Age of Reason, by belief in Mental Health and the expenditure of vast sums for 'fixing' the Other's mind (or 'problem'). Prayer for his victims/beneficiaries not only absolved the Man of Faith from guilt for his existential cannibalism, but made him positively proud of it. Similarly, the obligation and willingness to expend vast, tax-extorted sums on our victims/beneficiaries not only absolves us from guilt for our existential cannibalism, but makes us positively proud of it.

When people now debate whether psychoanalysis is or is not a science, they act as if they were talking about verifiability and falsifiability, when, in fact, they are talking about justifiability and legitimacy. Why do we ask or want to know whether psychoanalysis is or is not a science? To decide whether insurance companies should or should not pay for 'it'. And why should it make a difference to insurance companies whether a particular intervention called 'therapy' is or is not 'scientific'? Because only if it is scientific will the state recognize it as a 'legitimate treatment' and require insurance companies to cover the risk of needing it (and, to boot, make practitioners liable for tort damages if they do not provide such treatment to patients for whose 'diagnoses' it is 'appropriate'). Thus has the alliance of psychiatry and the state corrupted not only psychiatry and the state, but science itself.

Authorities—political as well as professional—legitimize their power by claiming that they are saving men, women, and children from one 'scourge' after another. During the nineteenth century and the first half of the twentieth, they saved us from sexual self-abuse (masturbation). Now they are saving us from chemical and existential self abuse (self-medication and suicide).

Affirmative action: Coercion in the name of justice. Involuntary psychiatric intervention: Coercion in the name of treatment.

The pen, the proverb tells us, is mightier than the sword. Of course: The sword needs the pen to legitimize it. The distinction between the *rightful* defense of God, Country, and Self and the *wrongful* killing of the innocent depends on the pen.

Authority legitimizes; the individual justifies.

Legitimacy rationalizes; rationality legitimizes.

Legitimacy is weakened by defiance: that is why it seeks consensus and compliance — by persuasion, if possible, by coercion, if necessary.

Rationality is strengthened by defiance: that is why it is indifferent to consensus and eschews coercion — and why its motto is 'A word to the wise is sufficient'.

The nineteenth-century intellectual saw more clearly the differences between legitimacy and rationality than does his modern counterpart. With the odor of sanctity lingering in his nostrils, he recognized that legitimacy, often tied to power, is likely to be coercive; whereas rationality, typically tied to knowledge, is unlikely to be so. In contrast, having replaced God with Reason, the modern intellectual, believing that rationality justifies legitimacy, resorts readily to the coercive control of those deemed to be irrational or unreasonable.

Perhaps better than anyone, Voltaire understood that only he who is legitimate can successfully wage war against the legitimizers. Asked by his secretary what he would have done had he lived in Spain under the Inquisition, Voltaire replied: "I would have worn a big rosary, and gone to mass every day and kissed all monks' sleeves, and tried to set fire to all their monasteries."[3] *Voilà l'homme!*

LIBERTY

In the classic Christian conception, liberty is freedom from the errors which obstruct the true knowledge of God. The man who completely rejects this freedom — exemplified by Nietzsche — is the 'mad *Übermensch*', the 'inhuman (superman) mental patient'.

In the post-enlightenment secular conception, liberty is freedom from the social conventions which obstruct true self-realization. The man who completely rejects this freedom — exemplified by Eichmann — is the 'sane *Unmensch*', the 'inhuman (non-man) bureaucrat'.

The person who wants to avoid the fanaticisms of both unconventionality and conventionality — that is, anyone who wants to live a decent life — must reconcile these opposing tendencies, and accept the tension between them as unresolvable.

Men love liberty because it protects them from control and humiliation by others, thus affording them the possibility of dignity; they loathe liberty because it throws them back on their own abilities and resources, thus confronting them with the possibility of insignificance.

Freedom is what many people want for themselves and few want for others.

The Russian people are profoundly ambivalent about living freely — deciding for themselves where and how to live. Because such a life seems too hard to them, they try to soften it by subjecting themselves to the ostensibly benevolent controls of political authorities. As a result they lead hard lives, devoid of freedom and dignity.

The American people are profoundly ambivalent about dying freely, deciding for themselves when and how to die. Because such a death seems too hard to them, they try to soften it by subjecting themselves to the ostensibly benevolent control of medical authorities. As a result, they die hard deaths, devoid of freedom and dignity.

Although Americans are more than a little ambivalent about the value of liberty in their own lives, they assume that other people, especially Russians, want more of it very badly. Nothing could be further from the truth. In the first place, it is reasonable to assume that if a people want to enjoy a good deal of personal freedom, they will, sooner or later, construct a social system consistent with that desire. The Russians have not done so. Moreover we now have opinion polls to support the supposition that the Russians place a low value on liberty. Thus, a poll conducted jointly by French and Russian sociologists in 1987 revealed that when asked "if they approved of the release of those who are called dissidents from prison or exile", 42 percent of the Muscovites responding said no. Asked if persons who want to leave Russia should be allowed to do so, "73 percent said they approved of giving exit visas to people who want to leave the Soviet Union"[1]: which means that slightly more than one out of every four Muscovites believes he should *not* have the freedom to leave his own country when he wants to. The idea that the very existence of an 'exit visa' is a violation of an inalienable human right has, I assume, not occurred to either the pollsters or their respondents.

If you truly yearn to be free, you must first recognize all the ways you are unfree. Only after constructing a complete catalogue of the constraints upon you can you begin to consider which ones you can and want to diminish or eliminate and at what cost (to you and others you cherish). Your self-liberation will be complete when you are left with constraints to which you willingly, perhaps even eagerly, submit.[2]

People—perhaps especially Americans, the myth of their love of liberty notwithstanding—have a passion for prohibiting all manner of human enterprises, even enterprises that are contractual and not harmful to third parties. For example, a mere twenty years ago (in 1968), it was illegal to: 1. Provide overnight mail delivery service or cable television service; 2. Own gold bullion; 3. Advertise, if you were a doctor or lawyer; 4. Operate a self-service gas station.[3]

While all of these enterprises have become legal since then, today it is illegal to: 1. Buy or sell most of the drugs people want (which had been available legally for

thousands of years, such as opium), or a hypodermic syr-
inge and needle (without a physician's prescription); 2. Pay
a person less than the 'minimum wage'; 3. Advertise a job
specifying that the applicant needs to be attractive or young;
4. Ride a motorcycle without wearing a helmet.

LOVE

The child loves out of dependency; the lover, out of desire; the newlywed, out of duty; the spouse and the parent, out of devotion; the long-married and the grandparent, out of habit.

The greatest joy in life is loving one's children; the next greatest, being loved by them. It follows that the greatest pain in life must be not loving one's children, and the next greatest, being unloved by them.

In the past parents and children *loved* each other; now they *bond*. That's progress?

Infants love the person who feeds them. We consider it a sign of maturity when children learn to love the food that relieves their hunger rather than the person who cooks or serves it.

In adults we reverse these judgements. Men and women are expected to love those who satisfy their sexual hunger.

And we consider it a sign of immaturity if they love not their sexual partners but only their partner's erotic attributes.

Men and women 'in love' share the mistaken belief that they live in the same world. They come to 'love' one another when they acknowledge that they live in different worlds, but are prepared, once in a while, to cross the chasm that separates them.

We should love our children more than they love us and even when they don't love us, because their self-esteem depends on our love more than ours depends on their love. But we should not love our spouses or lovers more than they love us, lest they misinterpret devotion as dependence.

MARRIAGE

Marriage: 1. A gift a man gives to a woman for which she never forgives him. 2. A legally binding contract which (at least for the first time) the contracting parties are expected to enter without legal assistance, but cannot exit without it. 3. Tenured togetherness.

Marriages are said to be made in Heaven, which may be why they don't work here on Earth.

Every marriage is an 'arrangement' between two persons. What else could it be? Hence, we should distinguish not between marriages and arrangements, but among different types of arrangements—marital and nonmarital.

Young love rests largely on loneliness and lust. This is why it is so poor a basis for marriage, which must rest largely on affection and respect.

Success or failure in marriage depends not on whether husband and wife love each other, but on whether they want to merge their lives and fortunes.

Trial marriage is to real marriage as buying and selling stocks on paper is to buying and selling them on the stock market.

A complex entity—such as a molecule, machine, or man—is (said to be) more than the sum of its parts. What complex whole is often less than the sum of its parts? A married couple.

A metaphor for many a modern marriage: Two competent swimmers in the water, safe but solitary, decide to play: one pretends to drown, the other to rescue; they grapple, sink, panic, and drown together.

Women marry hoping their husbands will change; men, hoping their wives won't. Bad enough, but couples can make it much worse by going to a psychiatrist to fix the problem.

By becoming 'one body' in marriage, wives can injure their husbands by eating too much and husbands can injure their wives by drinking too much. What psychiatrists call, and the public now accepts as, 'self-destructive' behavior is thus often the exact opposite: an attempt to preserve oneself by destroying what one regards as one's 'parasite'.

Alimony: Restitution payments to compensate the victims for the ravages of the war between the sexes.

In intimate human relations, psychological autonomy and physical proximity vary inversely. Those who want to maximize both — especially in marriage — will have neither; whereas those who are satisfied with one or the other, or some of each sometimes — as married people used to be and friends now tend to be — may have one or the other or sometimes some of each.

When a marriage becomes intensely unsatisfactory, the participants have a choice between breaking up and breaking down. Some prefer the former, others, the latter. Either solution is likely to generate new problems. The breakup of the marriage may lead to the breakdown of the wife or the husband; whereas the breakdown of the wife or the husband may lead to a much 'stronger' marriage, the sane member of the pair becoming the nurse-protector of his or her insane partner.

Monotheism and monogamy are based on the same

principle — exclusiveness. As a person can have only one
God, so he can have only one mate. Hence the violent op-
position, in Christian cultures, against both polytheism and
polygamy; and the intense possessiveness, both religious
and sexual, which people living in such cultures exhibit
toward their God and their mate.

Traditional (arranged) marriage was a fine institution
for legitimizing men and women as adults and for raising
children; it could be ruined, and was ruined, by one thing
only: the expectation that the participants enjoy each other
as sexual partners.

Modern (romantic) marriage is a fine institution for
legitimizing men and women as adults and for friendship
and sex; it can be ruined, and is ruined, by one thing only:
the expectation that the participants have children whom
they love and protect.

There are two ways of terminating an intense human at-
tachment, such as between husband and wife. One is to
draw up a set of grievances against one's partner, much as a
grand jury draws up a set of criminal indictments against a
defendant: The 'accuser' can then use these 'offenses' to
justify detaching himself from his partner. The other is to
resign oneself to being hopelessly mismatched with one's
partner and slowly to withdraw from feeling committed to
him (her): The relationship will then gradually wither
away.

MEDICINE

Formerly, when religion was strong and science weak, men mistook magic for medicine; now, when science is strong and religion weak, men mistake medicine for magic.

Formerly, a quack was someone who had fake cures for real diseases; now he is someone who claims to have real cures for fake diseases.

Formerly, people were duped by quacks because they believed in their fake cures; now, they are duped by them because they believe in their fake diseases.

Formerly, when our religion was Christianity, we fasted and feasted; now that it is Medicine, we diet and binge. Thus was gluttony replaced by obesity, prayer by psychotherapy, the monastery by the health spa, the clergyman by the clinician, the Vatican by the Food and Drug Administration, and God for whom being slim meant being virtuous by Medical Science for which it means being healthy.

Formerly, when religion ruled the mind of man, people believed in word magic: Prayer possessed boundless power to help man, and blasphemy boundless power to harm him.

Today, when medicine rules the mind of man, people believe in drug magic: medically prescribed chemicals possess boundless powers to cure, and medically prohibited chemicals boundless powers to corrupt.

The images of divine and devilish powers have thus remained the same; only the objects to which they are attributed have changed: from words in the Theological State, to drugs in the Therapeutic State.

We call the Pope 'pontiff', from the Latin *pontifex* or 'bridge builder' (from *pons* and *facere*), to signify that he is our ultimate bridge from this world to the next. Today, the physician is our pontiff — our bridge from a world without drugs to one with them. The *pontifex* enabled the dead soul to ascend to heaven; the modern physician enables the sick mind to ascend to health. Thus do we medicalize religion and re-theologize medicine.

Medicine cannot give meaning to life, but religion can. The modern tendency to theologize health is a pathetic attempt to cling simultaneously to the practices and promises of both religion and science. Often, the result is that people reap the bitterest fruits of both harvests.

What justifies a therapeutic intervention? For the true believer in medicine, the disease (which the alleged patient has); for the medical autocrat, the patient's (alleged) need for treatment; for the loyal medical agent of the Therapeutic State, the government's decision; and for the libertarian, the patient's consent.

Ignoring or confusing these conflicting moral and political premises is the source of most of our problems in medical ethics.

The most important distinction in the diagnostic vocabulary of medicine is that between symptom and sign. Typically, a symptom — for example, fatigue or pain — is said to be subjective; whereas a sign — for example, fever or high blood pressure — is said to be objective. Although this is a fair approximation to what is at stake here, the subjective/objective dichotomy may mislead. In fact, both symptoms and signs are *reports* a person makes about a *body*: A symptom is a report a person ('patient') makes about his own body; whereas a sign is a report a person ('physician', 'clinical pathologist', or other expert) makes about the patient's body. Symptoms no less than signs may be true or false. However, a symptom is more likely to be false in the sense that the patient's purpose is to deceive the listener, whereas a sign is more likely to be false in the sense that the reporter has made an unintentional error. For example, a laboratory technician may mix up two blood specimens and thus attribute James's anemia to John, but James is unlikely to erroneously attribute his headache to John, or vice versa.

If medical intervention is based on complaint, then the result must be measured in terms of the patient's satisfaction with it ('testimonial'). On the other hand, if medical intervention is based on lesion, then the result must be measured in terms of the physician's judgment of the effect of the procedure (lesion-removal and/or restoration of function). What is wrong with the former standard is exemplified by the fakeries of quacks that satisfy patients; what is wrong with the latter is exemplified by the old witticism that 'the operation was a success but the patient died'.

Some people believe that a person should have a right to kill himself: namely, that the intention (or alleged intention) to commit suicide should not be punishable by either the criminal or the mental hygiene law.

Others believe that a person should have a right to euthanasia: namely, that a physician, under certain circumstances, should be able to kill a person, unrestrained by the criminal law.

I support the right to suicide but not the right to euthanasia. However, I believe there is a right more fundamental than either — namely, the right to self-medication. Thus, the right, say, of a cancer patient, to take Laetrile or any other 'quack medicine' seems to me more elementary than his rights to suicide or euthanasia. Yet, this is the right physicians are the most eager to deny to patients.

A well person who claims to be sick and seeks medical care is said to be neurotic (typically, hypochondriacal); whereas a sick person who claims to be well and rejects medical care is said to be psychotic (typically, schizophrenic). These judgments reveal the self-interest of the physician: persons seeking 'unnecessary' medical attention are condemned slightly, whereas those shunning 'necessary' medical attention are condemned severely. In the medical ethic, the greatest crime the patient can commit is to reject the doctor; and the greatest crime the doctor can commit is to acknowledge that the person has a right to reject being a patient.

Genuine technical advances in medicine—such as the prevention of water- and food-borne infections, prophylactic inoculations, the use of antibiotics—are efficient but undramatic. Soon, people take their benefits for granted: The eradication (in advanced societies) of malaria, typhoid fever, trachoma, diphtheria has not made people happier or more grateful to their culture than they were in the past. In contrast, dramatic medical pseudo-advances—such as lobotomy for curing schizophrenia or transplanting the heart of a monkey into a man for curing heart failure—make people feel elated and impressed with the powers of medical science. This illustrates what the Romans had already clearly recognized—namely, that as soon as people have bread in their stomachs, they rank better circuses above better health.

Until recent times, a seriously ill person either recovered or died. Biotechnological advances have created three radically different outcomes of medical treatment and three correspondingly different aims for medical intervention: 1. To enable the patient to live as a socially functioning, self-respecting person; 2. to transform the person into a chronic ('professional') patient utterly dependent on doctors and others; and 3. to keep the patient alive as a quasi-cadaver on which physicians and medical technicians demonstrate their ability to keep organs and tissues alive.

Although no contemporary textbook of pathology mentions the word 'schizophrenia', much less recognizes or describes 'it' as a disease; and although medical researchers are ostensibly busying themselves trying to demonstrate that the (mis)behaviors psychiatrists call schizophrenia is a disease — the United States Government accepts 'it' not only as a disease, but as a disease susceptible to drug treatment: On October 20, 1989, *American Medical News* reported that "The Food and Drug Administration has announced approval of the use of a highly toxic drug to treat severe schizophrenia. . . . The drug, clozapine, was approved for use in patients who have not responded to at least two regimens of less toxic therapy."[1]

Patients suffering the torments of intractable pain due to terminal cancer who *want* heroin cannot get it — because the United States Government does not recognize heroin as a treatment. Patients infected with the HIV virus suffering the agonies of having an apparently untreatable illness who *want* drugs used abroad to treat AIDS cannot get them — because the FDA does not recognize such drugs as legitimate treatments. But individuals who *do not want* clozapine can get clozapine — and get it whether they want it or not.

This seeming paradox is emblematic of the politicization of modern American medicine: Paid by the State, the physician has rejected the idea that the aim of medicine is to succor the patient as a suffering *person* (and moral agent), and has embraced instead the idea that its aim is to treat an alleged disease (according to the rules laid down for it by government bureaucrats). In America today, the United States Government, not medical science, defines what is, and what is not, a disease or a treatment.

If you free a person of his obligation to pay for his treatment, you also deprive him of his right to define what constitutes treatment. Collectivistic planners for health care services, acting in defiance of the proverbial rule that 'he who pays the piper calls the tune', may sow the wind of medical idealism, but reap the whirlwind of medical indifference (or worse).

Today everyone claims to be working for the patient's best interests. No wonder the patient is in deep trouble.

The greatest analgesic, soporific, stimulant, tranquilizer, narcotic, and to some extent even antibiotic known to medical science—in short, the closest thing to a genuine panacea—is work.

MENTAL HOSPITAL

Mental hospitals: 1. The POW camps of our undeclared and unarticulated family wars. 2. Orphanages for adult 'orphans'. 3. Parking places for people who want to get out of the traffic jams of life. 4. Cemeteries for the living dead: dormitory beds are the gravesites; psychiatric diagnoses, the gravestones; psychiatrists, the gravediggers; patients, the corpses. In the literal cemetery, micro-organisms in the soil live off the tissues of the dead body; in the metaphorical cemetery, macro-organisms in the madhouse (called 'staff') live off the spirit of the living mental patient.

Medical hospitals are repair shops; mental hospitals, parking places.

Formerly, a child who had no parents (because they died or disappeared) was sent to an orphanage — not because people believed professional care was needed for a condition called 'orphanhood', but because the child could not take care of himself and no one else was able or willing to take care of him.

Today, an adult who does not take care of himself

(because he cannot or will not do so) is sent to a mental hospital — not because he does not take care of himself and no one else is able or willing to take care of him, but because people believe that he needs professional care for a condition called 'mental illness'.

Psychiatric emergency is to civil commitment as extortion is to taxation: The threat to harm oneself or someone else is a personal act of coercion, lacking political legitimacy and hence legal force; incarcerating a person in a mental hospital is a collective act of coercion, possessing political legitimacy and hence legal force.

No person confined in a mental hospital is free to leave. Nevertheless, the law distinguishes between two kinds of mental hospital patients: voluntary and involuntary. The voluntary patient thinks he can leave the hospital; he is wrong. The involuntary patient knows he cannot leave the hospital; he is right. Yet, because the voluntary mental patient has false beliefs convenient for the psychiatrist, while the involuntary mental patient has true beliefs inconvenient for him, psychiatrists insist that the former suffers from a mild mental disease, and the latter from a serious one.

Psychiatrists and psychiatric statisticians distinguish between voluntary and involuntary mental hospital patients. But so long as there are mental health laws authorizing the incarceration of persons under psychiatric auspices, there can be no voluntary mental hospital patients, just as there can be no voluntary taxpayers. (Perhaps some people would willingly support the State, just as they willingly support churches. But who they are, if any, cannot be ascertained so long as the person who does not pay 'voluntarily' is forced to pay a much heavier tax involuntarily.)

Involuntary mental hospitalization is like slavery. Refining the legal or psychiatric criteria for commitment is like prettifying the slave plantations. The problem is not how to improve or reform commitment, but how to abolish it.

MENTAL ILLNESS

A glossary:

Ambivalence: Mixed feelings.

Compulsion: Persistent, self-administered command.

Delusion: Belief said to be false by persons who do not share it.

Elation: Self-exultation and self-glorification.

Insanity: Insubordination to civilian authority.

Multiple personality: The many false faces of the person who does not show his one true face.

Narcissism: Conceit.

Obsession: Persistent self-administered idea, especially doubt or certainty.

Psychosis: Malignant seriousness manifested by inability to laugh at oneself.

Mental illness as caricature:

Depression: Contrition

Grandiosity: Conceit

Hypochrondriasis: Concern for being healthy

Mania: Decisiveness

Obsession-compulsion: Conscientiousness

Paranoia: Concern for danger and protection

Schizophrenia: Indolence

Mental illness as drama:

Depression: Tragedy

Hysteria: Melodrama

Mania: Comedy

Paranoia: Parody

Transvestism: Farce

Typically, bodily illness is something the patient *has*, whereas mental illness is something he *is* or *does*.

Bodily illness is in the patient's body; mental illness is in his record.

A person is said to *get* a cold, or *come down* with the flu, or *develop* cancer; but he *goes* mad. The verb 'go' again suggests that madness is a *doing*, not a *happening*.

Delusion of grandeur: Inflating one's self-esteem by self-created fictions; existential masturbation.

Delusion of worthlessness: The same as above; attributing cosmic significance to one's petty sinfulness.

In each case, real existential impotency is replaced by fake existential super-potency.

The person suffering from brain disease—say, Alzheimer's dementia—is like a fine building, once a comfortable home for families, falling into disrepair and becoming an empty shell, no longer fit for human habitation, whereas the person suffering from mental disease—say, schizophrenia, especially if he is an adolescent or young adult—is like an empty lot, for which a fine building was planned but never built.

Commitment laws invariably refer to the mental patient's 'dangerousness to himself and/or others', illustrating that, ontologically, mental illness is something the person *does* (to himself or others). This is why, if he wants to, a person can stop being mentally ill; and if he does not want to, no one can stop him from being mentally ill.

In the 1970s, in a dramatic show of pseudo-liberal largesse, psychiatrists gave their patients a 'right to refuse treatment'. It seems, however, that the effort to exercise that right is, itself, a mental illness requiring treatment. A conference at McGill University, in Montreal, in 1987, was entitled: 'Psychiatrist's Responsibility to Treat the Patient's Right to Refuse.'[1] Clearly, the Western idea of 'individual right' is just as foreign to western psychiatrists as it is to, say, Middle-Eastern religious fanatics.

Virtually, every bodily illness a person can have, a cadaver can have also. A cadaver may thus be said to have cancer, pneumonia, or myocardial infarction. But, surely, a cadaver cannot have a mental illness. Nevertheless, it is the official position of the American Medical Association, the American Psychiatric Association, and other medical and psychiatric groups that 'mental illness is like any other illness'.

According to contemporary scientific psychiatry, there are two kinds of mental disease: those whose neuropathological character has *already* been demonstrated to the satisfaction of pathologists, and those whose neuropathological character has *not yet* been so demonstrated. The former, called 'neurological diseases', are treated by neurologists; the latter, called 'psychiatric diseases', are treated by psychiatrists. Because this view now constitutes both scientific dogma and popular belief, the possibility that some psychiatric diseases are not diseases (but are only so called) is, *a priori*, ruled out of court.

Would-be medical patients are cautioned about medical treatments with the old adage that 'the cure may be worse than the disease'. Would-be psychiatric patients should be cautioned about psychiatric treatments with a new adage — namely, that 'there are no psychiatric diseases except those caused by psychiatric diagnoses and cures'.

"Madness," said Wittgenstein, "*need* not be regarded as an illness. Why shouldn't it be seen as sudden — more or less — change of character?"[2] Why not, indeed? Because we want to treat madness as an illness. It is as simple as that.

Psychiatrists say that the homosexual who doesn't like being a homosexual suffers from an illness called 'ego-dystonic homosexuality'. But psychiatrists do not say the Jew who doesn't like being Jewish suffers from an illness called 'ego-dystonic Judaism'; or that the woman who doesn't like being a woman suffers from an illness called 'ego-dystonic femininity'; or that the poor person who doesn't like being poor suffers from an illness called 'ego-dystonic poverty'.

Ostensibly, the American Psychiatric Association's *Diagnostic and Statistical Manual* is a list of mental diseases; actually, it is a list of the profession's claims to categories of conduct. As prospectors stake out claims for mines which, they suspect, harbor precious minerals, so psychiatrists stake out claims for madmen who, they suspect, harbor precious maladies. However, although minerals cannot own mines, madmen — being persons — can own madness. Thus, the only remedy for psychiatric imperialism is to restore madness to its rightful owner, the madman; and to give the psychiatrist access to it only on terms agreeable to the proprietor.

When a person fails to follow normal rules of conduct — that is, the rules most people follow — we say he is mentally ill, and when he does not respond to conventional rewards and punishments as we want him to respond — we say he is seriously mentally ill. It is true, of course, that one cannot treat many mentally ill persons 'normally'. But it is equally true that one cannot treat children, foreigners, the very old, the disabled, or the religious fanatic 'normally' either. The reason is simply that insofar as people live by different rules, have different expectations, respond to different rewards and punishments, they will consider each other immature, strange, bizarre, or crazy — and difficult or impossible to live with.

What people now call mental illness (especially in a legal context) is not a fact, but a strategy; not a condition, but a policy; not a disease the alleged patient has, but a decision which those who call him mentally ill make about how to act toward him.

Psychiatric diagnoses are stigmatizing labels phrased to resemble medical diagnoses, applied to persons whose behavior annoys or offends others. Those who suffer from and complain of their own behavior are usually classified as 'neurotic'; those whose behavior makes others suffer, and about whom others complain, are usually classified as 'psychotic'.

Illness, mental illness, race, religion, occupation: each is, *inter alia*, a personal characteristic or role — that may be assumed by a person or attributed to him. One of the features that distinguishes mental illness from medical illness — schizophrenia from diabetes — is that mental illness defines the person, whereas medical illness does not. This is why we read about 'schizophrenic murderers', but not about 'diabetic murderers'.

A woman kills her nine-month-old son because, she says, she believes that "The baby is the devil. . . . If I kill the demon, my husband will raise the baby to life again in three days and the world will know he is Jesus Christ."[3] Charged with first-degree murder, the mother is acquitted as not guilty by reason of insanity. She sues her obstetrician and the psychiatrist she had seen while she was pregnant.

Psychiatrists say she was suffering from 'postpartum psychosis'. I say she is colossally conceited.

What the psychiatrist calls a 'delusion of persecution' is one of the most dramatic human defenses against the feeling of personal insignificance and worthlessness. In fact, no one cares a hoot about Jones. He is an extra on the stage of life. But he wants to be a star. He cannot become one by making a fortune on the stock market or winning a Nobel prize. So he claims that the FBI or the Communists are watching his every move, are tapping his phone, and so forth. Why would they be doing this, unless Jones were a very important person? In short, the paranoid delusion is a problem to the patient's family, employers, and friends: to the patient, it is a solution to the problem of the meaning(lessness) of his life.

The proverb admonishes not to curse the darkness, but to light a candle. This seemingly good advice overlooks the advantages of cursing the darkness and not lighting a candle: namely, the benefit that comes from seeing oneself as a virtuous victim, and the justification for avoiding the consequences of vision. Thus are the patient's solutions the psychiatrist's problems.

For the mental patient's family and society, mental illness is a 'problem'; for the patient himself it is a 'solution'.

This was Freud's only discovery. Psychoanalysts now ignore it, and psychiatrists deny it.

The most basic human need is for relationship with other human beings. This need has been met primarily by and within the family (or clan), stabilized by religion and tradition. As conventional family ties have loosened and persons have become individuals, family relationships — as a source of human contact — have been replaced, in large part, by what we now call 'chronic mental illness'. We see — and conventionally are only supposed to see — the disutility of mental illness. Its utility — because of our unquestioned belief in the value of individualism — lies in binding together family members no longer bound by parental, marital, or filial ties.

Doubt is to certainty as neurosis is to psychosis. The neurotic is in doubt and has fears about persons and things; the psychotic has convictions and makes claims about them. In short, the neurotic has problems, the psychotic has solutions.

If a man lies about his car so he that can get more money for it, that is rational economic behavior; if he lies about himself so that he can get more attention, that is irrational madness. We respond to the former by bargaining about the price, to the latter by treating mental illness.

When a person does something dramatically bad—like shooting the President—it is immediately assumed that he might be mad, madness being thought of as a disease that might somehow explain why he did it. When a person does something dramatically good—like discovering how to prevent or cure a hitherto incurable disease—no similar assumption is made. I submit that no further evidence is needed to show that 'mental illness' is not the name of a biological condition whose nature awaits to be elucidated, but the name of a concept whose purpose is to obscure the obvious.

The search for the neuropathological correlates of mental illnesses is based on a fundamental misconception: namely, on viewing complex social performances as if they were simple reflex movements, like a grand mal seizure. We use terms such as 'schizophrenia', 'manic depression', and 'psychosis' to identify enduring patterns of human behavior that so-called patients exhibit and which the patients—or, more typically, their families and psychiatrists—find troubling and undesirable. Accordingly, psychopathological terms do not resemble neuropathological terms such as 'grand mal seizure' or 'locomotor ataxia', but instead resemble evaluative terms such as 'great statesman' or 'sadistic criminal'. Whether a person 'is' a statesman or a criminal depends partly on what he does and partly on our judgment of it as virtuous or wicked. Since the very phenomenon for which we seek a neuropathological correlate is an opinion—like whether a particular work of art is beautiful or not—it is *prima facie* absurd to look for 'its' neuropathological correlate. For what is the 'it' supposedly caused by a brain dysfunction?

The proposition that mental illness is not a medical but
a moral 'condition' (or idea) is evident from the fact that we
sever the 'mad criminal' from his crime, but do not sever the
'mad artist' from his art: We *discredit* the mad criminal as
lacking criminal intent and do not blame him for his criminal acts, but *credit* the mad artist with artistic intent and
praise him for his artistic acts.

"An Arkansas appeals court recently ruled that bipolar
disorder is a physical, not mental, illness." Comments Paul
Fink, M.D., President-elect of the American Psychiatric
Association: "The Arkansas case gives psychiatrists an ex-
traordinary window of opportunity . . . "[4]

It is deeply revealing of the nature of psychiatry that
psychiatrists look to the law, not science, to validate them
as scientists; to judges, not patients, to validate them as
healers. *Plus ça change* . . . . : Inquisitors looked to the
church to legitimize their fantasies as facts, and to the
prince to validate the torturing of bodies as the saving of
souls.

Sartre says that hysteria is a lie without a liar. One
could also say that the hysteric is a liar who does not admit
or recognize his lies.

As persons, we are both agents and storehouses of
memories. Our abilities as agents may be impaired—by
bodily injuries, illnesses, infirmities, and/or by legal and
political restraints. Similarly, our capacities as stores of

memories may be impaired — by bodily injuries, illnesses, infirmities, and/or by assaults on, and ablations of, our brains (the physical basis of our memories): sometimes, such assaults come from without, for example, from head injury or lobotomy; more often, they originate in the self and society, from a meeting of personal cowardliness with psychiatric coercion.

Freud said the hysteric suffers from reminiscences. Not so. The 'hysteric' suffers from his inability or unwillingness to come to terms with his ('traumatic') memories. The psychiatrist legitimizes this evasion, transforming it into an illness — and a mystery, which only he can unravel.

Similarly, the psychotic may be said to suffer from reminiscences: But again, it would be more accurate to say that he suffers from his inability or unwillingness to come to terms with his (guilty) memories — exemplified by Lady Macbeth. The psychiatrist legitimizes this evasion even more enthusiastically, transforming it into a serious illness — and a mysterious biological (genetic) defect, which only he can 'research'. In short, 'mental illness' is typically the result of a collusion between the individual, *qua* mental patient, and the psychiatrist, *qua* medical mystery worker — transforming the 'patient' from a person *qua* agent filled with memories, into a body *qua* receptacle filled with lesions. Patient and psychiatrist transform the bad memories into bad lesions and emerge with bad lives — the patient because he is deprived of integrity, the psychiatrist because his job is to help people to deprive themselves and others of integrity.

The 'paranoid' is a person who insists you don't like

him, when in fact you don't, but when the polite thing for him to do would be to keep quiet about it.

Among persons categorized as mentally ill, there are two radically different types. One is composed of inadequate, unskilled, lazy, or stupid persons; the other, of protesters, revolutionaries, those on strike against their relatives or society. Because psychiatrists do not differentiate between the unfit and the unwilling, they often attribute unfitness to unwillingness, and unwillingness to unfitness.

If a person doesn't listen to his inner voice when young, he may, before long, find himself 'hearing voices' which he'll think come from without.

Tyranny is forcing people — politically — to be unfree; insanity is forcing people — psychologically — to treat one as if he were unfree. The tyrant uses brute force to gain his way; the psychotic, the brutal drama of madness. The tyrant plays shepherd — forcing people to be sheep; the psychotic plays lost sheep — forcing people to be his shepherd.

Every *thing* — a landscape, a flower, a work of art — is a creation either of nature or of man; each may or may not be said to be beautiful. The beauty or ugliness of each is an attribution. Similarly, every *person* exhibits some sort of *behavior*; and every behavior, or person, may or may not be said to be mentally ill. The mental health or mental illness of each is an attribution. It may be a self-attribution, the person regarding himself as mentally ill; or it may be an attribution made by someone else, the person being defined as mentally ill by others.

The attribution of mental illness is both an accusation and an excuse. Which of these elements predominates in any particular situation depends on the context and its consequences; it cannot be inferred from the semantic use of the phrase 'mental illness'. This is why psychiatric (and other) accounts of persons characterized as mentally ill that omit any reference to who the person is, how and why he came to be so 'diagnosed', and what happened to him as a consequence are virtually meaningless: they are merely reaffirmations of the claim that mental illness *qua* illness is not a fiction but a fact.

Two great Englishmen have articulated — perhaps better than anyone could hope — the subject we now call 'mental illness'.

In 1651, Thomas Hobbes wrote:

> The passion, whose violence, or continuance, maketh madness, is either great vainglory; which is commonly called *pride*, and *self-conceit*; or great *dejection* of mind. . . . In sum, all passions that produce strange and unusual behaviour, are called by the general name of madness.[5]

In 1882, Samuel Butler wrote:

All our lives long, every day and every hour, we are engaged in
the process of accommodating our changed and unchanged selves
to changed and unchanged surroundings; living, in fact, is
nothing else than this process of accommodation; when we fail in
it a little we are stupid, when we fail flagrantly we are mad, when
we suspend it temporarily we sleep, when we give up the attempt
altogether we die.[6]

MONEY

Two proverbs that say nearly everything that needs to be said about money:

He who pays the piper, calls the tune.

People value what they pay for, and pay for what they value.

Financial analyses of the behavior of the stock market stand in the same relation to the behavior of the market as psychoanalytic interpretations of individual behavior stand to the behavior of individuals. Each is a fantasy of the interpreter/expert: attractive and plausible, if it appeals to the observer and confirms what he believes to be the case; absurd and ridiculous, if it repels him and disconfirms what he believes to be the case. Neither kind of analysis possesses the power to predict—whether the behavior of financial markets or of human beings; yet it is precisely a belief in this predictive power that makes people interested in such analyses.

MYTH OF MENTAL ILLNESS

Bodily illness is to mental illness as literal meaning is to metaphorical meaning.

We may be dissatisfied with television for two quite different reasons: because our set does not work, or because we dislike the program we are receiving. Similarly, we may be dissatisfied with ourselves for two quite different reasons: because our body does not work (bodily illness), or because we dislike our conduct (mental illness). We would be fools if we tried to get rid of beer commercials on television by having TV repairmen work on our sets. We are even more foolish when we try to get rid of phobias, obsessions, and delusions by having psychiatrists work on our brains (with drugs or electricity).

The bat flies through the air and looks like a bird—but is not a bird.

The whale swims in water and looks like a fish—but is not a fish.

The koala looks like a bear and is even called a bear ('koala bear')—but is not a bear.

Mental illnesses (may) look like diseases and are called diseases—but are not diseases.

Cancer and diabetes are literal diseases: no one in his right mind would claim they are not bodily diseases and ignore their somatic basis in the material structure of the human body.

Lovesickness and homesickness are metaphorical diseases: no one in his right mind would claim they are brain diseases and look for their somatic basis in the chemistry of nerve cells.

In which class do mental illnesses belong? Are they literal or metaphorical illnesses? It seems remarkable that simply because they are called 'mental illnesses'—or, more specifically, 'schizophrenia' or 'bipolar illness'—psychiatrists are certain that these are brain diseases and look for their somatic basis in the chemistry of nerve cells.

You are a psychiatrist. It's springtime. A young man comes to you complaining of boredom, fatigue, and lethargy. You diagnose spring fever and prescribe a drug (amphetamine). Soon the patient reports that he feels better and behaves better (whatever that means). You conclude that spring fever is a disease. (Doesn't the patient's response to the treatment prove it?)

You are a psychiatrist. A mother brings her son, in the springtime of his life, to you, complaining that he has dropped out of college and shows little interest in himself or his surroundings. You diagnose schizophrenia and prescribe a drug (Thorazine). Soon the mother reports that the patient feels better and behaves better (whatever that means). You conclude that schizophrenia is a disease. (Doesn't the patient's response to the treatment prove it?)

Mental illness is a neurochemical imbalance: Q.E.D.

If there is a logical class comprising items properly called 'diseases', *then* there must also be a class comprising items properly called 'non-diseases'. Moreover, because human beings are fallible, diseases must sometimes mistakenly be identified as non-diseases and vice versa: physicians call the first mistake 'missing an organic diagnosis', and the second, 'making a false diagnosis' (of a bodily disease the patient does not have). Finally, because human behavior is goal-directed, 'non-diseases' may sometimes be called 'diseases'. This may come about as a result of: 1. the metaphoric displacement of meaning, characteristic of ordinary language — as in the term 'lovesickness'; or 2. the strategic use of metaphor — as when a writer asserts that 'The white race is the cancer of mankind'; or 3. the conventional use of literalized metaphor — as when deviant behavior is called 'mental illness'.

Mental illness is a metaphor: For example, calling a pretended paralysis 'hysteria' (because it looks like a real paralysis due to bodily illness) is an instance of mental illness as a *phenomenal* metaphor; calling a murderer 'psychotic' (to justify acquitting him as insane) is an instance of mental illness as a *strategic* metaphor.

When physicians restore the life of a person whose heart has stopped, they prove that it is possible to *revive* a moribund person, not that it is possible to *resurrect* the dead. Similarly, were psychiatrists to discover that psychiatric patients suffer from neurological diseases, they would prove that mental patients have brain diseases, not that they have mental diseases.

We think that identifying a person as mentally ill is like identifying him as hypertensive, when in fact it is more like identifying him as ugly. Although there may be widespread agreement among members of a particular group or society with such a judgment, there is—and this is crucial—nothing objective or objectifiable about it (comparable, say, to a blood pressure measurement).

The patient with bodily illness, experiencing suffering, is driven to see a physician by pain; the patient with mental illness, making others suffer, is driven to see a psychiatrist by the police. The difference between bodily illness and mental illness is like the difference between the ways the word *driven* is used in these two sentences.

Looking for the organic etiology of mental illness is like looking for the caloric content of food for thought.

Trying to cure mental illness with brain surgery, electricity passed through the head, toxic chemicals, or any of the myriad other medically rationalized interventions is about as sensible and effective as trying to keep warm by chopping down and burning the family tree in the fireplace.

When we say that someone has 'no guts' we mean that he is a coward; we would consider it absurd to treat him with an intestinal transplant. When we say that someone has a 'nervous breakdown' we again mean that he is something like a coward, that he does not accept responsibility for the consequences of his ill-chosen or unlucky actions; but in this case we consider it eminently reasonable to treat him with hospitalization and drugs.

Literal diseases—such as malaria or melanoma—deprive the patient of life *without* the additional help of human agency: that is, pathogenic microorganisms or tumor cells are the agents of death. Metaphorical diseases—such as schizophrenia or manic-depression—deprive the patient of liberty and life only *with* the additional help of human agency: that is, the patient himself or another person are the agents of detention or death.

Literalization of the metaphor of mental illness, courtesy of the U.S. Patent and Trademark Office: "A chemical that can be injected into the body and scanned with X-rays for diagnosis of mental disease has been invented by two Georgetown University professors . . . Patent 4,716,225, granted this week, is assigned to the university. . . . Schizophrenia and manic-depression are among the ailments that can be detected with the method . . . "[1]

Indeed, brain diseases can — in principle always, in practice sometimes — be diagnosed by appropriate chemical and physical methods. But *mental* diseases?

If a person does not believe in God or heaven, it would be stupid for him to assert that prayer is ineffective for facilitating the trip to heaven. Similarly, if a person does not believe in mental illness or psychiatric treatment, it would be stupid for him to assert that antipsychotic drugs are ineffective for treating mental illness. Indeed, arguments of this type are counterproductive, each tacitly accepting a premise the speaker rejects — the reality of God and heaven in one case, of mental illness and psychiatric treatment in the other.

Thirty years ago I suggested that there is, and can be, no such thing as mental illness. Since then, with increasing frequency, psychiatrists have announced that this or that form of human behavior — for example, homosexuality — is not a mental illness. Such claims attract much popular attention, perhaps because they simultaneously assert and deny the validity of the concept of mental illness: By asserting that X is not a mental illness, they imply that although X *is not*, Y and Z *are*. As formerly people wanted both to believe and disbelieve in the existence of witches, so now they want both to believe and disbelieve in the existence of mental illness.

No sooner had my suggestion that mental illness is not a disease gained a measure of acceptance, than new suggestions were advanced as to what 'it' is. Thus, some psychiatrists maintain that mental illness is a form of brain disease; others, that it is a form of behavior to which individuals are driven by unbearably painful life experiences; still others, that it is a form of irrational or irresponsible behavior; and so on. Such attempts to rescue the term 'mental illness' are doomed to failure because they ignore the fact that emotionally charged terms have lives of their own and are not subject to fashionable enthusiasms for plastic reconstruction.

My suggestion that mental illness is not a disease was immediately and instinctively viewed as an attempt to redistribute the wealth inherent in madness — as if I were proposing taking it away from psychiatrists and giving it to psychologists. I intended nothing of the sort. Thinking or speaking of so-called mental illnesses as 'problems in living' or as 'personal problems' does not imply that these phenomena are the property of psychologists. Indeed, I have made it clear from the beginning of my work that the issue of control (or ownership) of conduct — healthy or sick, sane or insane — is an integral part of the problem of so-called mental illness, that in order to come to grips with this problem we must decide whether we value freedom more than health or vice versa, and that, because I value freedom more highly than health, I advocate returning illness and mental illness to their rightful owners—the patients and mental patients.

One of the arguments against my claim that there is no mental illness has hardened into a line that seems to convince people that I must be wrong. It goes like this: 'We believe in the medical approach to mental illness. There are others (and they may or may not mention me by name) who prefer the social approach. But they are wrong, because . . . '—and then they cite studies about the genetic determinants of schizophrenia or the effectiveness of drugs for controlling it.

I am often confronted with this argument, sometimes by reporters or others from the news media, and have concluded that it is founded on so successful a distortion of my position that it is virtually impossible to counter it. For if a well-meaning questioner does not see the point on which this riddle turns, no amount of fresh explanation about the mythology of mental illness is likely to make him see it. Still, I try to answer it, along this line.

'Let us go back four hundred years. Then people believed in witches, and the official explanation of witchcraft was theological. Now, suppose someone came along and said: "There are no witches. 'Witch' is merely a name we often attach to poor and helpless people, usually women." Would it be proper to call this person's position on witches a "social approach" to witchcraft as against the official "theological approach" to it? Of course not. What this person offers is not a sociological approach to witches, but a moral and philosophical criticism of the people who call other people "witches".'

Since everyone now knows that there are no witches, this explanation satisfies everyone about witchcraft. And since everyone now knows that there are mental diseases, this explanation satisfies no one about psychiatry.

Mental illness is a myth whose function is to disguise and thus render more palatable the bitter pill of moral conflicts in human relations. In asserting that there is no such thing as mental illness I do not deny that people have problems coping with life and each other.

My critics say that I 'deny the reality of mental illness', and cannot understand why I do not consider this an acceptable summary of my view. Would they consider it an acceptable summary of the conventional psychiatrist's view to assert that he 'adheres to the delusion that mental illness is like any other illness'?

A person planning to become an exorcist could not be expected to show much interest in the proposition that demonic possession is a myth. Faced with the possibility of the non-existence of possession, he would feel compelled to dismiss either the idea that possession is a myth or the idea of becoming an exorcist. Similar considerations obtain for the person expecting to profit from consulting an exorcist. (How can one be exorcised of non-existent demons?)

Mutatis mutandis, a person planning to become a psychiatrist cannot be expected to show much interest in the proposition that mental illness is a myth. Faced with the possibility of the non-existence of mental illness, he would feel compelled to dismiss either the idea that mental illness is a myth or the idea of becoming a psychiatrist. Similar considerations obtain for the person expecting to profit from consulting a psychiatrist. (How can one be cured of a non-existent mental illness?)

The moral: Although many people may feel, in their hearts, that there is no mental illness, few believe, in their heads, that they can afford to act as if that were true.

When everybody is convinced that something has a very high value—whether it be hunting witches in the sixteenth century, investing in tulip bulbs in the seventeenth century, or insisting that certain human desires or deeds are diseases in the twentieth century—there is no point in trying to get people to change their minds. But one does not have to go along. It is possible to resist the herd instinct, think for oneself—and not get hurt as the bubbles, relentlessly replenished with hot air, keep bursting.

For the past 25 years, one psychiatrist after another has dismissed my books, asserting that I repeat my 'one good idea'—namely, that mental illness is a myth. But if that is such a good idea, why don't psychiatrists accept it as valid?

Hearing me say that I don't believe in mental illness, people invariably ask: 'How, then, can you be a professor of psychiatry?' My answer: 'The same way that a person who does not believe in God can be a professor of religion. Such a person studies the history of various religions and the behavior of persons who believe in them; teaches about diverse religions and their particular claims and rules; and writes about his own reflections on all this. That is what I do with "mental illness".'

Having listened to or read my criticism of psychiatry, people often ask: 'Well, what do you suggest we do with the mental patients?' I offer a two-pronged answer:

Suppose that a person living in western Europe in the sixteenth century who believed that there were no witches and opposed burning them at the stake had been asked: 'Well, what do you suggest we do with the witches?' Obviously, he would have had to answer: Nothing. The same goes for the question about mental illness.

My point is that an institution (considered to be) essential for the integrity of society cannot simply be removed and replaced with something else. The only way to bring about such radical social change is by means of violent revolution, a method I reject both because it is violent and because it is counterproductive.

Accordingly, I believe I ought to confine my efforts to speaking and writing.

I can also offer a more practical answer, as follows. Insofar as the persons we call 'mental patients' are (or may be viewed) as losers, we could (should) do two quite different things for or to them, depending on what kinds of losers they are. The sore losers — that is those who, in their anger and frustration, deprive others of their lives, liberty, or property — should be punished with appropriate criminal penalties. The serene losers — that is, those who, despite their loss, respect the rights and dignity of others — could (should) be rewarded with appropriate consolation prizes. I might add that in such a hypothetical society — in which Psychiatry and the State would be radically separated — it would behoove the non-losers to accept the presence and suffering (if any) of the losers, without harming them in the name of helping them.

PERSONAL CONDUCT

A glossary:

Anxiety: The unwillingness to play even when the odds are for you.

Courage: The willingness to play even when the odds are against you.

Greatness: The willingness to expose one's littleness and risk embarrassment.

Happiness: An imaginary condition, formerly attributed by the living to the dead, now by adults to children, and by children to adults.

Reason: 1. The capacity to weigh and make choices. 2. The characteristic that distinguishes human beings from animals, and that human beings use to deny the validity of this distinction.

Boredom is the feeling that everything is a waste of time; serenity, that nothing is.

Clear thinking requires courage rather than intelligence.

If you don't listen to yourself, you won't hear what others say.

You don't have to be healthy to be happy.

There are two kinds of 'disabled' persons: Those who dwell on what they have lost and those who concentrate on what they have left. The former use their limitations as an excuse for parasitism, the latter, as an incentive for productivity. Helen Keller was much more impaired, but much less disabled, than many a modern professional schizophrenic.

Where does self-confidence end and conceit begin? Where dusk ends and night begins. In each case, an indistinct boundary demarcates a distinction as clear as that between white and black.

Knowledge is gained by learning; trust, by doubt; skill, by practice; and love, by love.

Every option is a risk, every risk an option.

As the price of liberty is vigilance, so the price of independence is self-determination, the price of dignity, self-assertion, and the price of respect, self-respect.

We spend most our time in one of two ways: making money or spending it. Only when we gamble can we do both at once, the proportion varying with our luck.

Obesity is to eating as promiscuity is to sex. For the religious, both are sins; for the therapeutic-statist, diseases; for the libertarian, the unhealthy and unesthetic consequences of overexercising the fundamental human right to one's self.

In economics, we speak of booms and busts; in psychiatry, of mania and melancholia. Both are the manifestations of human nature in a *state of freedom* — in particular, of the fact that, *unless adequately constrained by self-discipline*, the market fluctuates between manic highs fueled by greed and melancholic lows fueled by fear, while the individual fluctuates between self-assured, self-indulgent overactivity and self-doubting, self-loathing underactivity.

Literally, a victim is a person injured by another, for example, by a drunk driver. Metaphorically, a victim is a person injured by himself, for example, by drinking too much. Until recently, the metaphorical victim was regarded as a malefactor and was punished doubly: literally, by social sanctions imposed on him for his behavior, and metaphorically, by the biological consequences of his behavior. Now, the metaphorical victim is regarded as a literal victim—a patient disabled by an illness: instead of being punished for wickedness, he is compensated for sickness. The following is illustrative:

In March 1988, a Federal District Court in Florida ruled that a Federal employee "who drank a pint of gin a day [and] was dismissed from his job after missing . . . 389 days of work [in three years] . . . was legally crippled by alcoholism." The judge ordered the agency "to give him more than $150,000 in back pay" and ordered that the former employee be allowed "to apply again for his old job."[1]

Men diet to live longer; women, to look better.

There is no good digestion without hydrochloric acid, and no good thinking without adrenaline.

Self-control and self-esteem vary directly: The more self-esteem a person has, the greater, as a rule, is his desire, and ability, to control himself.

The desire to control others and self-esteem vary inversely: The less self-esteem a person has, the greater, as a rule, is his desire, and ability, to control others.

The proverb warns that 'You should not bite the hand that feeds you.' But perhaps you should, if it prevents you from feeding yourself.

People often say that this or that person has not yet found himself. But the self is not something one finds; it is something one creates.

'Where there is a will, there is a way,' says the proverb. Not entirely true; but it is true that where there is no will, there is no way.

The stupid neither forgive nor forget; the naive forgive and forget; the wise forgive but do not forget.

We pay too much attention to learning to acquire habits, and too little to learning how to break them.

Gratitude is contingent on a feeling of equality or

superiority. Men feel grateful not so much because others have treated them well (albeit this is usually a prerequisite), but rather because they have equalled or surpassed their former benefactor. The moral: expect gratitude only from those who, whether through your help or their own efforts, have equalled or surpassed you in life.

Men are often afraid to rock the boat in which they hope to drift safely through life's currents, when, actually, the boat is stuck on a sandbar. They would be better off to rock the boat and try to shake it loose, or, better still, jump in the water and swim for the shore.

Men cannot long survive without air, water, and sleep. Next in importance comes food. And close on its heels, solitude.

Solitary confinement is a severe punishment because people need other people. But people also need to be alone. For many persons, having to be with others is much more painful than having to be alone.

Formerly, men wanted to *do* a good job; from that desire arose craftsmanship. Today, they *want* a good job; from that desire arise unions and affirmative action programs.

Sooner or later, every person must ask himself: What should I make *of* my life? Which is the same as asking: What shall I make *in* it? One can make money, or machines, or food, or works of art, or children, or many other things. The person who feels or finds that he doesn't want to, or can't, make anything at all, can always fall back on making trouble—the product in which psychotics, psychiatrists, and politicians specialize.

One of the most important motives for personal conduct is the desire to avoid boredom. To satisfy this urge, men and women turn to food and drink, sex and work, crime and conquest.

Because it is easy, creating trouble for others is perhaps the most popular way of avoiding boredom. Creating trouble for oneself is a close second. Creating meaning in less dramatic and more constructive ways is more difficult and hence less popular.

Every American boy cannot become President; but every American boy can take a shot at the President. The road to fame is often closed, but the road to infamy is always open.

Like the proverbial cornered rat, the person who feels entrapped by life has three basic options: 1. He can kill himself. 2. He can kill someone else, compelling others to kill him or take care of him as a criminal. 3. He can go mad (by engaging in deviant behavior viewed as crazy), compelling others to take care of him as a mental patient.

A madman is one who has, or is alleged to have, lost control of himself; psychiatry supplies the justification for controlling him. The person securely in control of himself frustrates others from controlling him; hence, he is the object of both admiration and envy, awe and hate.

If someone does something we disapprove of, we regard him as bad if we believe we can deter him from persisting in his conduct, and as mad if we believe we cannot.

There would be less mental illness if fewer people believed in the sanctity of marriage and more believed in the sanctity of parenthood—specifically, in the parent's duty to take care of his children, especially when their welfare requires protecting them from a destructive mother (wife) or father (husband).

There are three categories of persons who can be counted on to break their promises: politicians, psychiatrists, and psychotics.

Psychiatrists and psychologists assert that in order to develop optimally, children need an optimal familial and social environment. Not so. Such an environment is necessary only for the development of plants and animals. To develop as persons, we do not need optimal familial and social conditions, which stunt rather than stimulate growth; instead, we need optimal obstacles whose successful mastery enriches us as competent performers and strengthens us as moral agents.

Most people want self-determination for themselves and subjection for others; some want subjection for everyone; only a few want self-determination for everyone.

If you don't value your family, you will not have a family that values you. If you don't value money or health or liberty, you will have no money or health or liberty. If you don't value knowledge and competence and self-reliance, no one, including yourself, will value you — and no amount of psychiatric treatment will remedy your failure to value what is worthy.

The masochist's maxim: It is better to be wanted as a victim than not to be wanted at all.

You can't teach an old dog new tricks; but you can an old man. That's one of the differences between dogs and persons.

Wherein lies the attraction, the excitement, the mystery of gambling? In a hitherto largely neglected characteristic of the gambler's experience: namely, his subjective sense of being in complete control of his decisions which is independent of his objective chances of winning or losing. Seemingly social, gambling is solitary: Although physically the gambler is in the presence of others, psychologically he is alone, uninfluenced by anyone. Like Walter Mitty, the gambler feels exhilarated by the experience of autonomous decision-making. This is why persons who feel constrained by others or their social circumstances tend to be attracted to gambling and may become hooked on it.

Success, people say, is not everything. Of course. But nothing is everything: No achievement, relationship, or possession can satisfy the restlessness of the human spirit.

Although his behavior may be utterly hypocritical, the man who professes unwavering belief in God and conventional wisdom is looked up to as a pillar of society; whereas the man who acts with absolute integrity but scoffs at religion and conventional wisdom is looked down on as a dangerous cynic.

Life is potentially a big empty hole and there are few more satisfying ways of filling it than by striving for and achieving excellence.

POLITICS

A glossary:

Conservative: 1. An autocrat — in the name of morality and tradition. 2. A believer in small government — just big enough to successfully impose his own values on others.

Liberal: 1. An autocrat — in the name of equality and social justice. 2. A believer in big government — just big enough to ensure fairness.

Libertarian: 1. A political oxymoron. 2. A believer in a government strong enough to protect people from external and internal enemies and weak enough to not threaten the autonomy of free and responsible individuals.

The State: A factory for fabricating falsehoods defined as truths by means of a monopoly on the 'legitimate' use of force.

Types of tyranny:

Economic: The authorities pauperize the people.

Political: The authorities enslave the people.

Psychiatric: The authorities invalidate the people.

The principal impediment to personal independence and political freedom lies, not surprisingly, in human nature: specifically in the fact that man possesses a powerful passion to control others; that the most effective way to do so is by infantilizing them and pretending to care for them; and that the most ineffective (indeed, counterproductive) way to do so is by respecting them and expecting them to care for themselves—which makes them independent and hence free of their benefactor's influence.

The year 1776 marks the publication of Adam Smith's *The Wealth of Nations* and the birth of the United States of America. Until then, the State was the director of the game of life and most people would have found it inconceivable that it could play any other role. With Smith and the Founding Fathers a radically new vision of politics came into the world: In this vision, individuals and groups of individuals are the proper players in the game of life, the ideal State functioning as umpire rather than player, much less director. While this has remained an unrealized and perhaps unrealizable idea, ever since, it has at least been clear that to the extent to which the State is a player, it is despotic and its principal enemy is individual liberty.

In the days of the Founding Fathers, the élitists were egalitarians. They did not fear making their inferiors their equals: embracing the free market, they saw their inferiors not only as potential competitors, but also as potential collaborators.

Today, the élitists are paternalists. They fear making their inferiors their equals: rejecting the free market, they see their inferiors only as potential competitors.

During the Middle Ages, when Christianity ruled the human mind, man was over-spiritualized — a situation exemplified by the Roman Catholic prohibitions against dissecting the dead and healing the sick by other than spiritual methods. The dominant ideology then proclaimed that the everlasting life of the spirit in heaven or hell was more important than the fleeting life of the body on earth, and people often behaved as if they believed it.

Today, when Scientism rules the human mind, man is over-animalized — exemplified by the scientifically established belief that abnormal (as well as normal) behavior can be explained by, and attributed to, chemical and physical processes in the brain and that mental illness annuls moral responsibility. The dominant ideology now proclaims that maintaining and prolonging the life of the visible and tangible body is more important than cultivating the integrity of the invisible and intangible human spirit, and people often behave as if they believe it.

Thus, there is now, as there was formerly, an imbalance between body and spirit, science and religion. Christianity was invaluable for raising man's moral sensibility and laying the foundation for individualism and freedom, but was worthless for advancing man's understanding and mastery of the physical universe (including his own body). Science is invaluable for advancing man's understanding and mastery of the physical universe, but is worthless for raising, or even maintaining, man's moral sensibility (or for helping him cope with novel ethical problems).

The two greatest enemies of the individual in the modern world are communism and psychiatry. Each wages a relentless war against that which makes a person an individual: communism against the ownership of property, psychiatry against the ownership of the self (mind and body). Communists criminalize the autonomous use of capital and labor, and harshly punish those who 'traffic' in the black market, especially in foreign currencies. Psychiatrists criminalize the autonomous use of the self, and harshly punish those who 'traffic' in self-abuse, especially in self-medication and self-destruction.

Addiction, obesity, self starvation (anorexia nervosa) are political problems: each condenses and expresses a contest between the individual and some other person or persons in his environment over the control of the individual's body and mind.

On all major vexing political and social issues of our day—the relations between blacks and whites; men and women; crime and punishment; drug abuse and the war on drugs; abortion, mental illness, and suicide—the contemporary (liberal) intellectual rejects clear, critical, principled thinking and resorts instead to pretentious psychobabble and sanctimonious compassion. The result is the economic destruction of his ostensible beneficiaries and his own spiritual self-destruction.

Masses of men can feel equally poor, but not equally rich. Hence, in proportion as we increase the importance of equality in human affairs, we inexorably diminish the importance of other values, such as liberty, responsibility, and justice. This, I believe, is the basis for the 'anticapitalist mentality' (von Mises) and the liberal infatuation with socialism (communism).

If Smith wants work but is unemployed, we (in the United States) don't accuse the government of depriving him of a job he needs; but if he wants treatment and goes untreated, we accuse the government of depriving him of medical services he needs. Thus, with respect to health care — which we supposedly value more highly than anything else in the world — we reject the capitalist mode of distributing goods and services and opt instead for the communist mode. In the long run, this choice probably poses a far greater threat to our liberty and 'American way of life' than does the military might of the Soviet Union.

Today, the Liberal acts as if only he felt compassion for the suffering of others. This is why blacks and women, the poor and the mentally ill believe that Democrats are their allies, and Republicans their adversaries. But no person or group has a monopoly on feeling compassion. Nor is the in-

tensity of feeling it politically relevant. The ability to experience compassion intensely (or the unverifiable but self-
flattering claim that one is intensely compassionate) does
not guarantee that one is especially competent to alleviate
the suffering of others. Indeed, all of history teaches us that
the persons most effective in relieving human suffering—men like Adam Smith or Thomas Edison—were relatively unconcerned with doing so; instead, they were con-
cerned with reducing certain basic causes of human suffering, especially the scarcity of goods and services.

What now plagues the masses of men and women in advanced industrial societies is a scarcity of meaning and self-
esteem—'goods' that cannot be supplied by others, or even
by oneself, once and for all; instead, they must be supplied
and resupplied for everyone by himself throughout his life.

The frequency and outcome of personal injury litigation
in the United States are best viewed as the manifestations of
a specifically American-capitalist method for redistributing
wealth—ironically, celebrating the Marxist maxim: 'From
each according to his ability, to each according to his need.'

In a modern mass democracy, such as the United States,
when the right man says the wrong thing, it is right; and
when the wrong man says the right thing, it is wrong.

In a modern totalitarian society, such as the Soviet
Union, only the right man, who is a spokesman for the Party, can speak, and what the Party says is right.[1]

People dream of making the virtuous powerful, so they can depend on them. Since they cannot do that, people choose to make the powerful virtuous, glorying in being victimized by them. After their secular savior — their Robespierre or Stalin — is safely in his grave, then the people glory once more in denouncing him as a betrayer of their trust. Then they repeat the cycle.

In the USSR, the religion of communism determines the mode of production; as a result, people lack consumer goods.

In the USA, the religion of therapeutism determines the management of crime; as a result, people lack safety in their homes and on the streets.

Jewish polity begins with the ancient Hebrews surrendering their freedom through the covenant between God and Abraham. English polity begins with the nobles asserting their rights through the Magna Carta. The Jewish and Anglo-Saxon people have been particularly thoughtful about the problem of man as a political animal — the former seeing the ideal person as God's favorite child, the latter seeing him as an independent adult, competing and cooperating with other adults. It is a great and dangerous foolishness to believe — as many Americans believe — that people who differ greatly in their religion and tradition nevertheless all want to live under the same sort of political system, and that that system is American-style democracy.

When you hear an American politician running for office say: 'I want to serve my country', remind yourself that what the man really means is: 'I want the country to be at my service.'

During election campaigns, the American people and press talk about nothing but how politicians lie and deceive the public. Once installed in office, both the people and the press treat politicians — and their lackeys who run government agencies — as if they were incapable of uttering a falsehood if their lives depended on it.

Ironically, the opposite generalization is closer to the mark. While campaigning, politicians tell us at least some of the truth (about their opponents) and thus warn us of the folly of trusting them. Once the election is over, however, no politician has any interest — for two, four, or six years, depending on the office he occupies — in uttering another honest word.

In the classic tale about the emperor's finely woven clothes, a child reveals that the emperor is unclothed. That makes him a naked emperor. The point of this story is not only that the emperor is naked, but that he is a liar, anxious to deceive both himself and others.

The corruptible politician is an evil, but the incorruptible politician is an even greater evil. Like a deity immune to propitiation by sacrifice, the politician incorruptible by bribe is more to be dreaded than desired. Only in a society governed perfectly by perfect rules of law would ironclad political incorruptibility be desirable. Since imperfect human beings cannot form such a society, political corruption is at once a bane and a blessing, in both free and totalitarian societies.

Today, there is an inverse relationship between the government's efforts to protect us from other people and from ourselves: The more compassionately politicians try to protect people from harming themselves, the more callously they fail to protect them from being harmed by others. The upshot is a system of government ever more zealous to protect us from driving cars without seatbelts or ingesting 'illicit' substances, leaving us ever more unprotected against murderers and polluters.

The collectivist looks to the state to prohibit what he considers to be self-harming practices (for example, consent to electroshock treatment); whereas the individualist looks to the individual to protect himself from such practices. Inasmuch as anti-psychiatrists advocate state control of psychiatric practices they disapprove, they are—despite their seeming agreements with my criticisms of psychiatry—collectivists. This is what makes our disagreements more important than our agreements.

Modern monarchs reign, but do not rule. Modern mental patients have rights, but not liberty.

Personal generosity: Willingly giving what belongs to oneself and doing so selflessly, even anonymously. Typical of selfish capitalists and individualists.

Political generosity: Coercing others to give what belongs to them, claiming credit for helping the needy, and compelling the beneficiaries to pay personal and political homage to the coercer. Typical of selfless anti-capitalists and collectivists.

People can identify and sympathize with the suffering of a persecuted individual, but not with that of a persecuted group. The fate of a victim, like Alfred Dreyfus or Anne Frank, has generated more concern and compassion than have the fates of millions of victimized Armenians or Jews. This is why politicians persecute groups, not individuals; and this is why politicians are so dangerous.

Juvenal (60–c. 130) summed up the central problem of political tyranny with this immortal question: *"Quis custodiet ipsos custodes?"* ('Who shall guard the guardians?'). History, as I read it, has answered his question with a resounding: 'No one'. Advocates of parliamentarianism in England and of the separation of governmental powers in the United States have tried to solve the problem by creating several guardians to guard one another. But it hasn't worked that way. Instead, what has happened is that each guardian, in his own way, has tyrannized over the people. I conclude that if people truly want to safeguard their personal liberty and responsibility, then they must limit their own expectations of the guardian's duties: They should expect him to guard them against external and internal enemies, but not against themselves.

"It is error alone," wrote Jefferson, "which needs the support of government. Truth can stand by itself."[2] One could invert this and assert that it is error alone which can support government. Because truth can stand by itself, it has no need for government; and because it has no need for government, truth is fundamentally inimical to government.

To the politician who supports the interventionist state, responsibility means that it is his duty to control people and the market: When he does, he feels responsible; when he doesn't, he feels negligent. Telling himself he helps people to be secure and the markets to be stable, he (perhaps) disguises his own need to be in control as concern for the common good.

To the politician who supports the free market, responsibility means that it is his duty to leave people and the market alone: When he does, he feels responsible; when he doesn't, he feels meddlesome. Telling himself that he helps people to be responsible and the market to be free, he

(perhaps) disguises his own need to be left alone as respect
for the autonomy of the individual.

Most people cannot accept the human condition — that
is, the actual physical and spiritual nature of man. Man's
inability to accept himself as a physical being is manifested
by the denial of death and the affirmation, as a reality, of
life in the hereafter. Man's inability to accept himself as a
spiritual being is manifested by the denial of human diversity and depravity and the affirmation, as a reality, of the
fundamental uniformity and decency of human nature
(spoiled only by demons or mental diseases). Not until
educated persons accepted the finiteness of their physical
selves could anything resembling a science of medicine
come into being. *Mutatis mutandis*, not until most
educated persons accept the spiritual diversity and potential
depravity of human beings, can we begin to contemplate a
civilized and peaceful ordering of society — maximally
tolerant of personal differences and scrupulously protective
of individual rights.

The plague of mankind is the fear and rejection of diversity: monotheism, monarchy, monogamy — and, in our
age, monomedicine. The belief that there is only one right
way to live — only one right way to regulate religious,
political, sexual, medical affairs — is the root cause of the
greatest threat to man: members of his own species, bent on
ensuring his salvation, security, and sanity.

As no two persons have the same fingerprint, so no two persons have the same self-interest. Sellers want to give the least for the most; buyers want to get the most for the least. Only in the marketplace are both the seller and the buyer compelled to compromise and co-operate if they want to do business — that is, if they want to realize their aspirations; this is what makes free exchange in the market the most moral economic relationship. Introducing fraud — and, especially, force — into this relationship destroys the balance between the participants, annuls their choice, and hence their liberty and individuality. What is the point of satisfying human wants if it is achieved at the cost of sacrificing what makes human beings human?

Until modern times, scapegoats were deprived of life, liberty, and property. Poor women, called witches, were put to death. Rich Jewish merchants, called Christ-killers or well-poisoners, were dispossessed and usually deprived of their liberties and lives as well.

Since the end of the Second World War, we, Americans, have developed a new way of using our scapegoats: instead of *taking* away their life, liberty, or property, we *give* them entitlements. For example, poor inner-city males are entitled to high school diplomas (even if they are illiterate), and to commit crimes (while the police look the other way); poor inner-city females are entitled to produce babies (without having to take care of them), and to make money as mothers (without mothering anyone). In short, the modern American scapegoat is not persecuted; he is pampered. The scapegoater's goal is not to liquidate him, but to render him into an object of loathing. Instead of eliminating the scapegoat from the body politic, he is now incorporated into it as an irreparably defective subhuman object that provides lucrative work and self-enhancing worry for a vast corps of social fixers and professional weepers whose task is to encourage the scapegoats to respect their disreputable selves.

"Sometimes it is said," warned Thomas Jefferson, "that man cannot be trusted with the government of himself. Can he, then, be trusted with the government of others?"[3]

There is thus a fundamental contradiction between a system of government based on the people's choice of their elected representatives, and a deterministic psychiatry based on the premise that people are incapable of rational choice.

PSYCHIATRY

A glossary:

Deinstitutionalization: Reinforcing the subjection of the mental patient by substituting psychiatric tutelage for psychiatric terror.

Insanity plea: Psychiatric alibi based on the scientization of Christianity; evil deeds formerly attributed to demonic possession are now attributed to 'irresistible impulses' or 'schizophrenia'.

Legal insanity: The disease caused by committing a crime and being caught; its precipitating cause is the trial; its diagnosis is the verdict; and its treatment is incarceration in a hospital for the criminally insane.

Medical model: When psychiatrists speak about the medical model for psychiatry, they mean one or more of the following propositions:

that so called mental diseases are proven or putative brain diseases;

that regardless of what so-called mental diseases are, they ought to be treated as if they were (brain) diseases;

that so-called mental diseases are medical problems and

hence only physicians (psychiatrists) ought to be allowed to treat persons suffering from such diseases.

that because so-called mental patients are dangerous to themselves and others, and because they do not know what is in their own best interests, compulsory measures may legitimately be used to restrain and treat them.

Psychiatric diagnosis: The psychiatrist's statement about the patient, useful for the psychiatrist.

Psychiatric expert testimony: Mendacity masquerading as medicine.

Psychiatric nosology: A dictionary of defamations disguised as diagnoses.

Psychiatric symptom: The patient's statement about himself, translated into psychiatric jargon useful for the psychiatrist.

Psychiatric training: The ritualized indoctrination of the young physician into the theory and practice of psychiatric violence.

Psychiatrist: A person trained in medicine which he doesn't practice, practicing psychotherapy in which he is not trained.

Psychiatry: 1. Conflicts without adversaries. 2. An ostensibly medical discipline whose subject matter is neither minds nor mental diseases, but lies. These lies begin with the names of the participants in the transaction — the designation of one party as 'patient' even though he is not ill, and of the other as 'therapist' even though he is not treating any illness; they continue with the lies that comprise the subject matter of the discipline—the psychiatric 'diagnoses', 'prognoses', and 'treatments' and they end with the lies that, like shadows, follow ex-mental patients through the rest of their lives—the records of denigrations called 'depression', 'schizophrenia', or whatnot, and of imprisonments called 'hospitalization'. If we wished to give psychiatry an honest name, we could call it 'mendacitology', or the study and practice of lies.

Psychohistory: The vilification of hated, and glorification of loved, historical figures—presented as the products of impartial psychiatric-historical research.

Psychopathology: Problems in living renamed as mental diseases.

Psychotherapy: The psychiatric mystification and management of problems in living renamed as treatments.

Psychosomatic medicine: The medical philosophy according to which bodily diseases are mental, and mental diseases, physical.

There are two kinds of psychiatry: voluntary and involuntary, contractual and institutional. To confuse them is like confusing ally and adversary, freedom and slavery.

The crucial distinction between contractual and institutional psychiatry is being rapidly eroded. The psychiatrist's social mandate to control the patient (dangerous to himself or others) increasingly vitiates his effort (should he even want to make it) to serve as his patient's agent. Voluntary psychiatry is thus becoming an anachronism; while involuntary psychiatry—increasingly disguised as, and confused with, voluntary psychiatry—is becoming the medical-legal standard for what constitutes professionally proper psychiatric practice.

The relationship between the psychoanalyst and his client is exquisitely co-operative, between the psychiatrist and his committed paranoid patient implacably antagonistic. These diametrically opposite 'therapeutic encounters' are both subsumed within the boundaries of the same discipline. That psychiatrists expect the same physicians to practice both 'methods' testifies to psychiatry's lack of professional integrity: that laymen accept the psychiatrists' pretending to do so testifies to the non-psychiatrists' thoughtlessness about psychiatry.

Institutional psychiatry is the result of the marriage of unemployables: The patients are unemployable lay persons; the psychiatrists, unemployable physicians. Having joined them in holy madness, the state blesses their union and supports those so united.

Why does the state do so? Because by exiling patient and psychiatrist into the domain of mental illness and institutional psychiatry, society is enabled to contain both madness and mad-doctoring. Institutional psychiatry thus fulfills a basic human need—to validate the self as good (sane) by invalidating the other as evil (insane). This arrangement is at once the reason for, and a consequence of, the fact that mad persons and mad-doctors have something crucial in common—namely, that neither is able or willing to perform services saleable in the free market. The madman produces complaints and self-neglect, the mad-doctor contempt and constraints—'products' unsaleable in the free market.

There are, and can be, no abuses of institutional psychiatry, because institutional psychiatry is, itself, an abuse; just as there were, and could be, no abuses of the Inquisition, because the Inquisition was, itself, an abuse. The Inquisition was the characteristic and perhaps inevitable abuse of Christianity; institutional psychiatry is the characteristic and perhaps inevitable abuse of medicine.

"War," said Randolph Bourne, "is the health of the state."[1] What did Bourne mean? That war is the ultimate *raison d'être* of the state, the rhetoric of 'protecting the national interest' justifying a virtually unlimited extension of the size and scope of governmental activities. The sense of national emergency engendered by war transforms the destruction of dissident opinion into patriotism.

Similarly, psychosis is the health of psychiatry. Why? Because psychosis is the ultimate *raison d'être* of psychiatry, the rhetoric of 'protecting the patient's best interests' justifying a virtually unlimited extension of the size and scope of therapeutic activities. The sense of psychiatric emergency engendered by psychosis transforms the deprivation of liberty into hospitalization and therapy.

In the Age of Faith, the Scapegoat was defined in religious terms: he was the arch-sinner, the Devil, the anti-God, the anti-Christ, the Jew as Christ-killer (Religious [Christian] anti-Semitism).

In the Age of Science, the Scapegoat is defined in medical terms: he (it) is the arch-disease, the plague, the addiction, the Jew as pathogenic agent in the body politic (Therapeutic [National Socialist] anti-Semitism).

In the Age of Faith, the institution entrusted with waging the struggle against the Scapegoat was Religion: this is what made the Church the principal adversary of individual liberty, dignity, and responsibility.

In the Age of Science, the institution entrusted with waging the struggle against the Scapegoat is Medicine: this is what makes Psychiatry the principal adversary of individual liberty, dignity, and responsibility.

Institutional psychiatry offers solutions to problems of housing by camouflaging them as problems of health: it defines some of the homeless as 'mentally ill', confines them in institutions called 'hospitals', and justifies forcible incarceration and decarceration as 'medical treatment'.

The latest obscenity in the long history of institutional psychiatry is the forcible eviction of the chronic mental patient from the hospital that has become his home. In the United States today, individuals who want to stay out of mental hospitals are still 'admitted' to them against their will; whereas individuals who want to stay in such hospitals are now also 'discharged' from them against their will. The result is that while the prison function of the mental hospital has remained unchanged, its asylum function has become progressively eroded.

The doctrine of the 'right to treatment', enthusiastically embraced by self-seeking public-interest lawyers in the 1960s, has led, in the 1980s, to the denial of asylum, deceptively called 'deinstitutionalization'.

Like the term 'mental hospitalization', the term 'deinstitutionalization' is pure fraud—a euphemism disguising reality.

The term 'mental hospitalization' conceals the fact that it stands for a confused and confusing mixture of incarcerating persons who are unable or unwilling to take care of themselves (who may be offensive into the bargain), and persons who engage in violent and other criminal acts. The term 'deinstitutionalization' similarly conceals the fact that it stands for a confused and confusing mixture of forcibly relocating persons housed in mental hospitals in other tax-supported domiciles under mental health auspices, and forcibly evicting persons housed in mental hospitals with the expectation that they will live on the streets.

After the defeat of the Germans in World War II, we did not speak of the deinstitutionalization of Jews. After the defeat of the Japanese, we did not speak of the deinstitutionalization of Japanese-Americans. These people were simply freed: the shackles imposed on them by their adversaries were removed and they were restored to the same status—possessing the same rights and responsibilities—as their liberators. So long as the self-styled psychiatric protectors of mental patients are unwilling to do the same for persons denominated as mental patients—that is, abolish civil commitment and the insanity defense—there can be no meaningful discussion either of how we might most effectively protect, or how we might most appropriately punish, individuals we now call 'insane'.

Why are Soviet 'psychiatric abuses' abuses? Because they entail psychiatric interventions imposed on patients against their will? No, it cannot be that, because we, in the free West, also impose psychiatric interventions on patients against their will.

Is it because they entail imposing psychiatric interventions on persons against their will even though the so-called mental patients are, in fact, not mentally ill? No, it cannot be that either, because the persons subjected to involuntary psychiatric treatments in the Soviet Union are mentally ill by Soviet psychiatric criteria, just as the persons subjected to such interventions in the United States are mentally ill by American psychiatric criteria.

Is it, then, because we view some of the persons the Russians call 'schizophrenics' as 'dissidents'? Yes. We thus come down to the issue of legitimizing the particular application of abstract criteria for justifying psychiatric coercion, which vary, of course, depending on the legitimizer's interests and values (which is why involuntarily hospitalized mental patients typically consider their own confinement unjustified, but consider the confinement of other 'crazies' justified).

"I myself spent nine years in an insane asylum," wrote Antonin Artaud, "and I never had the obsession of suicide, but I know that each conversation with a psychiatrist, every morning at the time of his visit, made me want to hang myself, realizing that I would not be able to cut this throat."[2]

On the other hand, Vincent Van Gogh wrote: "I am thinking of frankly accepting my role of madman, as Degas took the character of a notary . . . For the time being I wish to remain shut up [in an insane asylum] . . . Where I have to follow a rule, as here in the hospital, I feel at peace . . . "[3]

Would patients other than psychiatric patients say such things? If the answer is no, does that not tell us precisely what we most need to, and least want to, know about psychiatry?

When out of power, politicians promise to do good; when in power, they do well instead. Similarly, when they were out of power, psychiatrists promised to humanize medicine; when they gained power, they medicalized the humanities instead.

Biological psychiatrists, firmly committed to the support of coercive psychiatric practices, assert that I dehumanize mental patients when I suggest that their delusions may be lies or pretenses. However, only human beings lie; indeed, lying is a characteristic feature of the behavior of politicians, priests, and psychiatrists—individuals whose status as moral agents we never question. Hence, to place delusional mental patients in the same class with such respected liars acknowledges and affirms their humanity, rather than denying or impugning it.

To the psychiatrist, the patient's lies are delusions. In abolishing the lie, he abolishes language and in abolishing language, he abolishes man—as C. S. Lewis warned that he would.

A well-worn joke among psychiatric house-staff goes as follows: 'We had a serious emergency last night. We had to commit God. Why? Because he had the delusion he was . . . (name of the chief of psychiatry).' If psychiatrists acknowledged what this joke at once reveals and conceals—namely, that a person is confined in an insane asylum when he no longer knows his place—they could not, in good conscience, continue to practice psychiatry.

The scapegoater accuses a person of a wrong he did not commit; the psychiatrist forgives and punishes him for it.

In pre-Freudian psychiatry, sex was repressed; in post-Freudian psychiatry, power is.

We often hear and read about 'escaped mental patients' committing murder or suicide or engaging in other newsworthy activities. But who has ever heard of or read about 'escaped diabetes patients' or 'escaped cancer patients' doing such things?

In the seventeenth and eighteenth centuries, when men like Hobbes and Jefferson talked about the church, virtually everyone understood that they were talking about politics (power), not religion (morality). Today, when presidents, governors, senators, and other politicians talk about psychiatry, virtually no one understands that they are talking about politics (power), not medicine (healing). My point is that English and American politicians assume, and are expected to assume, that the power of priestcraft is evil, and hence they oppose it—whereas they assume, and are expected to assume, that the power of psychiatry is good, and hence they support it. So long as this remains true, there can be no genuine psychiatric reform.

The characteristic inconsistency and intellectual dishonesty of anti-psychiatrists and their followers: asserting that *psychopathology* (mental illness) is not real (literal) disease, but that *psychotherapy* (conversation) is real (literal) treatment.

The characteristic inconsistency and intellectual dishonesty of ex-mental patients and their so-called liberation movement: rejecting the attribution of mental illness to a person in order to deprive him of *liberty*, but accepting such an attribution in order to excuse him of *responsibility* for his criminal behavior.

Psychiatrists are in a hopeless fix: They cannot become honest professionals so long as they pretend to be physicians diagnosing and treating mental diseases; but if they frankly acknowledge that they are advocates and adversaries in human conflicts, then they cannot hope to be accepted as physicians.

Talmudic scholars prefer studying and practicing the exegetics of God's Word to attending to man's humanity and inhumanity to man. Psychiatrists prefer studying and practicing the exegetics of DSM-III to attending to what persons designated as mental patients and psychiatrists say and do to one another.

The man who kills for his country and wants to avoid working needs only to say '*I cannot forget* (what I did in Vietnam)'; immediately, psychiatrists rush to testify under oath that he is disabled by his memories and suffers from post-traumtic stress disorder.

The man who kills his countrymen and wants to avoid going to jail needs only to say: '*I cannot remember* (what I did in Vermont)'; immediately, psychiatrists rush to testify under oath that he is disabled by his lack of memory and suffers from dissociative reaction or schizophrenia or some other ominous mental illness.

Cui bono? Advance a claim of remembering too much or too little and, presto, we are off to the psychiatric races.

The first thing to remember about mental health policy is that we speak of 'policy' only when goods and services are allocated by the government rather than exchanged in the free market. (We speak of a 'policy' for feeding Africans, but not for feeding African violets.) As 'defense policy' or 'foreign policy' can serve only the interests of a collectivity (the nation), so 'mental health policy', too, can serve only the interests of a group (and cannot serve those of particular individuals, as they themselves would define their self-interests). Is it any wonder that the more we talk about 'mental health policy' and the more tax monies we spend on 'mental health care', the larger our 'mental health' problems grow?

Psychiatrists now treat the same mental illness both with electrically induced convulsions and with anticonvulsant drugs; which is as if physicians treated the same disease with blood-letting and blood transfusion. This paradox is a paradigm of what counts in psychiatric treatment: not good sense, empirical proof, respect for the patient's consent — but the brazen imitation of doctors, sensationalism, and contempt for the patient as a person.

Freud said that psychoanalysis helps the patient to exchange neurotic misery for ordinary unhappiness. *Mutatis mutandis*, organic-psychiatric treatments help the patient to exchange ordinary unhappiness for the miseries of psychiatric cures.

Formerly, priests burned men's bodies to save their souls. Today, psychiatrists imprison men's bodies to save their minds.

Some people make bad jokes *out* of their lives; others make bad jokes *about* them. The former are the psychotics; the latter, the psychiatrists.

In the Soviet Union there is no formal censorship of the press. It would be wrong to conclude, however, that the press is free: On the contrary, the 'censors' write and publish the newspapers. A similar situation prevails in the United States with respect to psychiatric information.

According to Lewis L. Judd, the director of the National Institute of Mental Health, "The whole premise [of psychiatry] now is that profoundly disordered behavior is a psychobiological phenomenon. It manifests itself in behavior, but it's got to be related to dysfunctional mechanisms in the brain."[4]

This, of course, is merely a restatement, in contemporary language, of the classic belief of alienists that mental illnesses are brain diseases. Because all behavior must be 'related' to the brain, the premise that disordered behavior is related to *dysfunctional* brain mechanisms implies that not-disordered behavior is related to *functional* brain mechanisms. But this cannot be true because the human brain is essentially the same in different cultures, but what counts as 'profoundly disordered behavior' is not.

"Surviving spouses' depression studied", announces a typical headline ballyhooing new psychiatric research.[5] To understand the true nature of psychiatry we need to do no more than realize, and take seriously, the absurdity and impossibility of a headline announcing: "Surviving spouses' elation studied".

Present-day psychiatric thought and rhetoric rest on three implicit assumptions: 1. That every kind of undesirable behavior (harmful to oneself or others) is an instance of mental illness; 2. that every mental illness is the result and symptom of brain disease (proven or provable by future medical technology); and 3. that every person afflicted with a mental illness is, potentially, a legitimate subject for involuntary mental hospitalization and treatment.

Doctors control diseases, not persons; psychiatrists control persons, not diseases.

"Superstition is to religion," wrote Voltaire, "what astrology is to astronomy — the very foolish daughter to a very wise mother."[6] Just so is psychiatry to medicine.

Psychiatry is the sewer into which modern societies discharge their insoluble moral and social problems. As sewers pollute the waters into which they empty, so psychiatry, emptying into medicine, pollutes the care and cure of the sick.

The business of psychiatry is to provide society with excuses disguised as diagnoses, and with coercions justified as treatments.

As an old psychiatric joke has it, the neurotic builds castles in the air, the psychotic lives in them, and the psychiatrist collects the rent. I would add that the psychiatrist builds a profession and prisons on a metaphor, the neurotic seeks solace in them, and the psychotic is sentenced to them.

Human beings exist in two states of conciousness: asleep and awake. Psychiatry may be used to make persons either more asleep or more awake: chemotherapy as well as psychotherapy may either sedate or stimulate the patient—depending on the nature of the drug he ingests and the nature of the conversation in which he engages.

The psychotic lacks personal self-esteem; like Lady Macbeth, such an individual cannot, for good reasons, admire himself as a person; hence, he must manufacture imaginary grounds for self-esteem or perish.

The psychiatrist lacks professional self-esteem; like a confidence man, such an individual cannot, for good reasons, admire himself as a physician; hence, he, too, must manufacture imaginary grounds for self-esteem or perish. The psychiatrist knows he doesn't belong in medicine. That is why he became a psychiatrist. Finding that he now has no place to live, like the deinstitutionalized mental patient, he is eager to return to the institution.

Thus do psychotic and psychiatrist fabricate their insane delusions and their medical theories of insanity, each as fantastic as the other, each as impervious to refutation by logical reasoning or empirical evidence as the other.

There are students who don't study and mothers who don't mother, but there are no patients who are not sick. The 'patient' who has no bodily illness is considered to have a mental illness.

With increasing zeal, psychiatrists insist that mental

diseases are brain diseases. They do not seem to realize that
the logical consequences of this claim are as inimical to the
welfare of psychiatry as a profession as are the consequences of my claim that mental illness is a myth. Here is
why.

Neurology is the medical specialty devoted to the
study, diagnosis, and treatment of diseases of the nervous
system (brain, spinal cord, peripheral nerves). Psychiatry is
the medical specialty devoted to the study, diagnosis, and
treatment of diseases of the mind (schizophrenia, depression, substance abuse, and so forth). If mental diseases are
brain diseases, then psychiatry would (should) be a part of
neurology. And if scientific and judicial authorities would
recognize this to be true, medical schools would (should)
teach neurology, but not psychiatry; courts would (should)
recognize neurology, but not psychiatry; and the government and insurance companies would (should) pay for the
treatment of neurological illnesses, but not for the treatment of mental illnesses.

"Ideology," in Minogue's apt formulation, "is a form of
theoretical conscription: *everyone*, by virtue of class, sex,
race or nation, is smartly uniformed and assigned to one
side or the other."[7] But Minogue omitted one of the most
important contemporary criteria for classifying persons:
mental health/mental illness. This is what I mean when I
assert that psychiatry is an ideology.

The ostensible agenda of psychiatry is diagnosing and
treating patients suffering from mental diseases. Its real

agenda is treating mental patients like criminals, and criminals like mental patients—degrading both, and depriving both of liberty and responsibility.

Responding to criticisms of their practices, Soviet psychiatrists objected to the idea of "including patients in treatment decisions . . . [because] in psychiatry and the rest of medicine it is not the accepted custom [in the Soviet Union] to discuss with patients the methods for treating them, except for cases where the physician is the patient." Nevertheless, "the Soviet psychiatric officials acknowledged that their laws need provisions for informed consent to treatment . . . ."[8] Welcome to the Alice-in-Wonderland world of American-Soviet psychiatric relations.

Critics of psychiatry who agitate for abolishing one or another psychiatric practice (or the whole profession) are even more dangerous enemies of individual liberty and responsibility than the psychiatrists they oppose. The scope of discrete psychiatric procedures—such as lobotomy, electroshock, or psychotherapy—is, after all, limited to those who voluntarily submit to them or can be coerced to be victimized by it. However, the abolition of any particular procedure limits the choice of every member of society and undermines the fundamental concept of the individual as a competent adult who can manage his life without the meddling of a Protective State. Moreover, the demand to abolish, say, electroshock treatment replaces a legitimate object for state control with an illegitimate object for such control: it is the duty of the State (in a free society) to protect people from *coercion*, and to leave them alone to enter into *voluntary* contracts with one another.

Accordingly, the patient must be protected from the coercion of the psychiatrist (conventionally called 'treatment'), and the psychiatrist must be protected from the coercion of the patient (conventionally called 'symptom'). It is stupid to speak of 'involuntary psychiatric treatments' when what we mean are psychiatrically rationalized assaults; or to speak of 'violent patients', when what we mean are persons who commit violent crimes. And it is stupider still to constrain contract and hence abridge individual liberty and responsibility and claim to be doing so in an effort to combat violence.

A free adult in a free society gets something because he *wants* it, is willing to *pay* for it, and finds someone willing to *sell* it to him. In contrast, a child gets something because he *needs* it, is willing to *cry* or *beg* for it, and finds someone, or more often simply finds himself in the presence of someone, who is willing to *give* it to him.

Patients, especially mental patients, rarely if ever get what they want, especially if they ask for it. For example, were a person to ask a psychiatrist (or psychiatric hospital) for room and board; for benzodiazepines or electric shock treatment; or to be discharged—he would receive none of these services. He would, however, get all this, and much else, were he to properly (conventionally) deceive the dispensers of services into believing that he, the 'patient', *needs* them or *requires* them. For example, if he threatens to kill himself or slashes his wrist and has the police bring him to the emergency room, he will receive room and board; if he complains of panic and sleeplessness, he will receive Xanax or Dalmane; and if he behaves as if there were nothing the matter with him and confides, in confidence, to a friendly nurse, how he is ripping off the mental health system, he will receive a discharge.

In short, there is a fundamental disjunction in the mental health system (and there has always been) between what the provider of services thinks the patient needs or requires ('therapy'), and what the recipient wants or requests (which may be being left alone by the psychiatric authorities or a service totally different from what the providers want to give him). The result is mutual manipulation, defense, and aggression — each party trying to get the better of the other. What is missing is collaboration and co-operation, precisely the ingredients in the absence of which it is a travesty to speak of 'therapy', much less decency and respect.

The two necessary preconditions for the contractual/ non-coercive practice of psychiatry (the secular cure of souls): 1. Abolition of involuntary mental hospitalization (repeal of all civil and criminal commitment laws); 2. Separation of psychiatry and the state (in particular, prohibiting the state from funding mental health services as it is prohibited from funding religious services).

My psychiatric critics angrily accuse me of wanting to destroy psychiatry. But what is wrong with advocating a psychiatry in which the psychiatrist can't do anything to the patient which the patient doesn't want done to him?

The power of an idea whose time has come is said to be

irresistible. Today, mental illness is such an idea. This is why I believe that the problem with psychiatry is not so much that psychiatrists have too much power—though they do; it is rather that the idea of mental illness has too much power—given to it by the people who believe in it. Thus, only when people withdraw their blind faith in mental health and mental illness will they see fit to curb the powers of psychiatry—just as only when people withdrew their blind faith in God and the Devil did they see fit to curb the powers of priestcraft. The kind of power psychiatrists now wield is similar to the kind of power priests wielded before the Enlightenment: it does not come out of the barrel of a gun held by an oppressor; it comes out of beliefs held by human beings who prefer to rely on mystifying symbols and paternalistic authorities rather than on themselves.

Colleagues often tell me that they chose to become psychiatrists because they felt they were all screwed up and thought that it would help them put their heads on straight. They ask me why, since I am 'hostile' to psychiatry, I chose to become a psychiatrist. I tell them: because I felt psychiatry was all screwed up and I thought I could put its head on straight.

PSYCHOANALYSIS

A glossary:

Free association: The term used by the psychoanalyst to register his approval of the patient who talks about what the analyst wants him to talk about.

Freud on Freud: "I am actually not at all a man of science, not an observer, not an experimenter, not a thinker. I am by temperament nothing but a conquistador — an adventurer . . . "[1]

Libido theory: the litany of the Freudian services.

Psychoanalysis: 1. The trade name of a certain kind of conversation (just as Coca-Cola and Kentucky Fried Chicken are the trade names of a certain kind of soft drink and fast food). 2. The name of a body of speculations about life and human relations put forward by the originator of the trade name. 3. The only medical specialty in which one must be a patient before one can become a therapist. (Which is like requiring that a physician be a cancer patient before becoming an oncologist, or that he be a dead patient before becoming a pathologist. Although such a requirement is alien to medicine, it is familiar in religion. The strength of Christianity, Christian Science, Alcoholics Anonymous, and other religious movements rests heavily on their recruiting members from among those saved by one or another of these sects.)

Psychoanalytic diagnosis: " . . . just let all the millionairesses stay crazy, they don't have anything else to do."[2]

Psychoanalytic gigolo: Male psychoanalyst kept by and exploiting his wealthy female patient; the psychoanalytic equivalent of (a man) marrying for money; virtually the only way for a psychoanalyst, (nominally) *qua* analyst, to make a significant amount of money.

Psychoanalytic institute: A school where the faculty, composed of middle-aged and old men and women, systemically degrades and infantilizes the students, composed of psychiatrists fast approaching middle age, who eagerly submit to this degradation ceremony in the expectation, often unfulfilled, that, after being deprived of all independent judgment and the capacity to form such judgment, they will be able to inflict a similar treatment on others, call it psychoanalysis, and charge high fees for it.

Psychoanalytic meeting: The Yom Kippur service of the secularized and scientific faithful: instead of regaling God in Hebrew with accounts of their own spiritual sinfulness, the worshipers regale each other, in the jargon of psychoanalysis, with accounts of the mental sickness of their patients.

Psychoanalytic theory: The work song of the Freudian boatmen.

Psychoanalytic treatment: " . . . talking people into and

out of things—which is what my occupation consists in . . ."3

Resistance: 1. The term the psychoanalyst uses to register his disapproval of the patient who talks about what he himself wants to talk about. 2. The patient's reluctance to keep paying the analyst for a service the patient no longer finds useful.

Training analyst: 1. A nonswimmer working as a lifeguard. 2. An optician fitting his patient with distorting lenses.

The Unconscious: 1. The promised land of the psychoanalytic faithful. 2. The territory of a psychoanalytic Mafia.

The term *psychoanalysis* is a strategically literalized metaphor—devised and developed to make it seem as if the psyche were like blood or urine and could be 'analyzed'. Playing this language game for all it's worth, some psychiatrists have duly claimed to have invented 'psychosynthesis'.

Freud converted speech into a specimen—to be analyzed by means of the fake technique of free association: dreams into dung—the excrement of the mental apparatus in which the analyst as laboratory technician searches for the pathological contents of the patient's unconscious mind; and legendary heroes, like Oedipus, into 'complexes'—

henceforth to serve as the labels of mankind's innate and incurable insanities. In short, Freud medicalized and thus
dehumanized language, history, and the whole of human
existence.

Psychoanalysis now serves as a language for concealing
and repressing the existence of moral conflicts and choices,
just as formerly Latin served as a language for concealing
and repressing the existence of sexual body parts and performances.

Freud gave the right account of psychoanalysis, but
placed it in the wrong category: he described it as a type of
contract and conversation, but classified it as a type of
treatment. This is one of the reasons for the hopeless confu-
sion and controversy about whether or not psychoanalysis
is a type of medical practice: when couched in the language
of medicine — as a treatment for an illness — it belongs, by
definition, to medicine; and when couched in the language
of communication and contract — as a conversation about a
persons' past and present experiences and methods of coping with his life — it clearly doesn't belong to medicine.

Freud was like Ford: Each developed a better mouse-
trap — Freud for lunacy, Ford for locomotion. However, in
insisting that psychoanalysis was not conversation but
a special type of treatment, Freud made a claim as patently
false and fraudulent as Ford's claim would have been had
he insisted that the Model-T was not a car but a special type

of horse. Freud's achievement thus lay not in any discovery, but in the ability to make people accept his classification of the car as a horse—of conversation as treatment.

"The moment a man questions the meaning and value of life," declared Freud, "he is sick, since objectively neither has any existence; by asking this question one is merely admitting to a store of unsatisfied libido to which something else must have happened, a kind of fermentation leading to sadness and depression."[4]

This assertion sums up Freud's effort to medicalize morality, and hence all of life: Because life *is* morality, through and through, just as language *is* metaphoric, through and through. Freud's life and work—exemplified by the above quotation—illustrates this.

Psychoanalysis is a modern, pseudo-scientific version of Judaism. The Orthodox Jew believes the Jews are the Chosen People; the Orthodox Psychoanalyst, that 'training' analysts are the Healthy People.

Freud and the Freudians deprived Jung of many of his best ideas and, to boot, defamed him as an anti-Semite. Actually, Jung was more candid and correct than Freud in identifying psychotherapy as an ethical rather than technical enterprise; and Freud was more anti-Christian than Jung was anti-Jewish.

Psychoanalysis is a religion disguised as a science: As
Abraham received the Laws of God from Jehovah to whom
he claimed to have had special access, so Freud received the
Laws of Psychology from the Unconscious to which he
claimed to have had special access.

Pleasure in genital eroticism is literal sexuality. Pleasure
in eating, defecating, urinating, and so forth is metaphorical sexuality. In his theories of sexuality, Freud first met-
aphorized human pleasure and then literalized his own
metaphors, insisting that nonsexual pleasures are not merely *like* sexual pleasures, but *are* sexual pleasures.

Freud viewed sex in the same anti-erotic way as the
Church fathers before him did—that is, as either procreation or pathology. The Church fathers saw sex as dangerous temptation, weakness, and sin—or babies; the
father of psychoanalysis saw it as masturbation, venereal
disease, and perversion—or babies. In short, Freud had not
the slightest understanding of sex as legitimate lust, as personal adventure, and as the potential locus for exceptional
intimacy and respect between man and woman.

The psychoanalyst sees all behavior as the Puritan sees
sex: intellectually, he replaces the subject's enjoyment of his
behavior by the authority's explanation of it; practically, he
uses his explanation as a justification for condemning, for-
bidding, or otherwise regulating the subject's behavior. In

short, although psychoanalysis seemingly sexualizes behavior, actually it puritanizes it.

The eucharist stands in the same relation to a snack of bread and wine as psychoanalytic treatment stands to ordinary conversation. The fact that the Host is bread is overshadowed, in the mind of the faithful, by the awe and respect he feels for the Church. Similarly, the fact that psychoanalysis is conversation is overshadowed, in the mind of the faithful, by the awe and respect he feels for Medicine.

Confession is to free association as absolution is to interpretation, as holy water is to cigar smoke, as original sin is to the Oedipus complex, as the soul is to the mental apparatus, as the priest is to the psychoanalyst, as Jesus is to Freud.

The priest puts the penitent on his knees; the psychoanalyst puts the patient on his back. In each case, the physical arrangement of the encounter symbolizes the dominant theme of the transaction between the participants: the priest wants to make the penitent feel humbled; the psychoanalyst wants to make the patient feel helpless. Having imposed 'original sin' on the penitent and induced 'transference neurosis' in the patient, priest and psychoanalyst can proceed to rescue the one from sin and the other from sickness and demand their eternal gratitude for having 'saved' them.

Psychoanalysis is an attempt to examine a person's self-justifications. Hence, it can be undertaken only with the patient's co-operation and can succeed only when the patient has something to gain by abandoning or modifying his system of self-justification.

The analyst should be a catalyst, facilitating the patient's communication and confrontation with himself: he should mediate between the patient's acknowledged and unacknowledged desires and decisions. The analyst does not change the patient, but helps the patient to change himself. This is one of the reasons why an outsider to the psychoanalytic situation can never know why a patient has not changed as a result of analysis: the analyst might have failed to give the patient the proper kind of help, or the patient might have preferred to remain as he was.

The satirist deflates personal pomposities by ridiculing them: his method is laughter. The psychoanalyst inflates personal problems by solemnizing them: his method is lamentation. The satirist ridicules folly, but respects it; he laughs, lest he weep. The psychoanalyst diagnoses folly and debases it; he weeps, lest he laugh. The former is 'hateful' toward those he satirizes, but treats them as equals;

the latter is 'loving' toward those he analyzes, but treats them as inferiors.

Humorless persons make poor patients; humorless therapists make pathetic analysts.

Beware of the psychoanalyst who analyzes jokes rather than laughs at them.

Psychology

Intelligence test: Hocus-pocus used by psychologists to prove that they are smart and their clients stupid. The general acceptance of these tests suggests that this claim may not be without foundation.

Projective tests: Hocus-pocus used by psychologists to prove that they are normal and their clients abnormal. The popular acceptance of these tests suggests that this claim, too, may not be without foundation.

There is no psychology; there is only biography and autobiography.

PSYCHOTHERAPY

Psychotherapy is a myth: Psychotherapeutic interventions are metaphorical treatments that stand in the same relation to medical treatments as editing television programs stand to repairing television sets.

Psychotherapy is a metaphor: For example, calling advising persons how to manage their spouses 'marriage therapy' (because it looks like advising them how to manage their diabetes) is an instance of psychotherapy as a *phenomenal metaphor*; calling imprisoning persons 'hospitalization' (to justify it as a psychiatric intervention) is an instance of psychotherapy as a *strategic metaphor*.

As mental illness is not something the patient *has* (in his body or mind), but something he *does* (especially what he says) — so psychotherapy is not something the therapist *has* (to give the patient), but something he *does* (especially with and about the patient).

Architects design houses, not homes; homes are what people create, or fail to create, out of their houses. Similarly, psychotherapists provide conversations, not cures; cures (of souls, now called 'successful psychotherapies') are what clients who engage in such conversations create, or fail to create, out of their contacts with psychotherapists.

The psychotherapist who calls his conversations with clients 'patient-interviews' and tape records them is like the traveler who calls strange places and people 'tourist attractions' and 'natives' and photographs them. Each puts a technological barrier, a gadget, between himself and his own experience, thus attenuating or killing it, while at the same time telling himself that he is trying to preserve it for more perfect future recall.

But by objectifying and recording his experience each destroys precisely that which ostensibly he tries to preserve.

As one man's meat is another man's poison, so one man's psychotherapy is another man's psychopathology.

Psychotherapists used to be called 'mental healers'.[1] Which raises the question: Are mental healers like brain healers — that is, neurologists and neurosurgeons? Or like faith healers — that is, ministers (engaged in the 'cure of souls') and charlatans (selling the proverbial snake oil)? Psychiatrists claim that (medical) psychotherapists are brain healers; I maintain that they are faith healers.

(Whether they are charlatans or not depends on what they do and claim they do.)

The term *psychotherapy* denotes diverse principles and practices of ethics couched in the idiom of treatment; each reflects the aspirations and values of its practitioners. Classifying psychotherapies according to what the therapist expects from the patient, we can distinguish three general types:

1. *Compassionate* therapy — the therapist expecting improvement and gratitude: 'Get well.' 2. *Commanding* therapy — the therapist expecting obedience and awe: 'Do what I tell you.' 3. *Contractual* therapy — the therapist expecting payment and reciprocity: 'Listen to yourself, trust yourself, and I shall try to help you change your life if and as you want it changed.'

People seeking help from psychotherapists can be divided into two groups: those who wish to confront their problems and change their lives by changing themselves; and those who wish to avoid the inevitable consequences of their life strategies through 'therapy'. The former are likely to benefit from therapy in a short time; the latter are likely to mark time for years or even decades and sink ever deeper into their self-created existential morass.

Samuel Butler began to write *The Way of All Flesh*[2] in 1872 and completed it in 1884, about the same time that

Sigmund Freud began to show interest in psychotherapy (and some ten years before the publication of Breuer and Freud's *Studies on Hysteria*[3]). In the following passage, Butler anticipates what we now call the 'medical model' of mental illness and psychotherapy:

> Rome has reduced the treatment of the human soul to a science, while our own Church, though so much purer in many respects, has no organized system either of diagnosis or pathology — I mean, of course, spiritual diagnosis and spiritual pathology. Our Church does not prescribe remedies upon any settled system, and what is still worse, even when her physicians have according to their lights ascertained the disease and pointed out the remedy, she has no discipline which will ensure its being actually applied. If our patients do not choose to do as we tell them, we cannot make them. Perhaps really under all the circumstances this is as well, for we are spiritually mere horse doctors as compared with the Roman priesthood, . . . either the priest is indeed a spiritual guide, as being able to show people how they ought to live better than they can find out themselves, or he is nothing at all — he has no *raison d'être*. If the priest is not as much a healer and director of men's souls as a physician is of their bodies, what is he? The history of all ages has shown that as men cannot cure the bodies of their patients if they have not been properly trained in hospitals under skilled teachers, so neither can souls be cured of their more hidden ailments without the help of men who are skilled in soul craft — or in other words, of priests.
>
> As for men curing themselves, . . . they can no more cure their own souls than they can cure their own bodies, or manage their own law affairs. In these last two cases they see the folly of meddling with their own cases clearly enough, and go to a professional adviser as a matter of course; surely a man's soul is at once a more difficult and intricate matter to treat, and at the same time it is more important to him that it should be treated rightly than that either his body or his money should be so.[4]

Butler used the 'medical model' as an explicitly

analogical device to explain the function of the priest as spiritual guide. Freud labored mightily, and successfully, to turn this analogy into an identity—that is, to define psychoanalysis as a literal treatment, except when it suited his political-polemical purposes to disavow this transparent literalization of a metaphor:

> I have assumed that psychoanalysis is not a specialized branch of medicine. . . . The words, "secular pastoral worker," might well serve as a general formula for describing the function of the analyst.[5]

Nevertheless, Freud never stopped hoping that he would receive the Nobel Prize in medicine, to which he felt fully entitled by his great 'discovery'.

Like a Renaissance pope preaching celibacy by day and sleeping with concubines at night, Freud preached strict adherence to 'analytic' rules which he himself steadfastly violated. This sort of hypocrisy, which may well be a requirement for becoming a religious leader, ill becomes anyone who respects others, especially those who seek his help. A decent psychotherapist should set rules only for himself, which he should follow. If others want to emulate his behavior, that is their affair, not his; how others practice psychotherapy is none of his business (except as an observer of, and commentator on, the human condition).

Indeed, why would a psychotherapist want to formulate rules for other therapists to follow? How would the successful propagation of such rules benefit him, except by aggrandizing him as a great rule-maker? But making rules for others is, *par excellence,* an enterprise in heteronomy, incompatible with advocating autonomy.

The autonomous psychotherapist's role *vis-à-vis* his client is like the court jester's *vis-à-vis* the monarch: the therapist confronts the client with painful reality, in as friendly a way as possible; the client retains complete control over whether or not he wants to listen to the therapist.

People with personal problems often behave like the proverbial drunk who looks for his house key under the streetlight, not because that's where he dropped it, but because that's where the light is. Should such a person consult an autonomous psychotherapist, the therapist's job is not to try to find the key, but to suggest to the patient that he light a match or borrow a flashlight from a neighbor and go look for his key where he dropped it.

Success in psychotherapy — that is, the ability to change oneself in a direction in which one wants to change — requires courage rather than insight.

Hypnosis: Two people lying to each other, each pretending to believe both his own and his partner's lies.

For psychiatrists, mental illness is brain disease; for psychologists, behavioral disorder; for social workers, family (or 'system') problem. However much these mental health professionals might disagree on *what* they are treating, they all agree that psychotherapy is an effective *therapeutic* intervention and that their particular brand of it is the best.

The most popular and financially successful psychotherapists in the United States today are the faith healers — the Oral Robertses, Jerry Falwells, Jim and Tammy Bakkers. Far more money pours into the coffers of clerical than clinical healers. Indeed, the clinician in the psychotherapy business is to the entrepreneur in the guru business as the chef in an elegant French restaurant is to the owner of a chain of fast food establishments.

During the 1950s and 1960s, when psychoanalysis was fashionable, the title of a typical psychiatric article or lecture was: 'The Psychodynamics of Depression'; today, when psychopharmacology is fashionable, a typical title is 'The Drug Treatment of Depression'.

Formerly, psychiatrists wanted to demonstrate the reason the patient is depressed; now they want to demonstrate that there is no reason for him to be depressed. Then, 'insight' was believed to be therapeutic for 'it'; now 'drugs' are believed to be therapeutic for 'it'.

Is there a cure for depression? In the medical sense, no;

in the existential sense, yes. When the person's depressing life situation improves (because of his own actions or for any other reason), his depression will disappear.

Before the Enlightenment, religious truth was accepted as a justification for coercion; since then, psychiatric truth has been so regarded. The former view illustrates the mind-set that sees controlling deviants in the name of God as unquestionably good; the latter illustrates the mind-set that sees controlling deviants in the name of mental health in the same way. Let us keep in mind that we in the West have long repudiated the legitimacy of violence in the name of God. So long as we do not similarly repudiate the legitimacy of violence in the name of Mental Health, the terms 'psychiatric help' and 'psychiatric reform' will carry an impossible load of ambivalence, rendering them useless, if not obscene.

Voltaire said: "No priest should ever deprive a citizen of the least prerogative on the pretext that this citizen is a sinner, because [the priest] . . . should pray for other sinners, and not judge them."[6] This maxim defines the role of the autonomous psychotherapist, who must abide by the principle that 'No psychotherapist should ever deprive a citizen of the least prerogative on the pretext that this citizen is mentally ill, because the psychotherapist should only listen and talk to his patients, and not deprive them of liberty or responsibility.'

Legally, psychotherapeutic practices should be treated as sexual relations are. If the relationship is consensual, both (or all) parties engaging in it voluntarily, the therapy should be permissible; it is no one else's business whether the therapy is good or bad, helpful or unhelpful. On the other hand, if the relationship is coerced, the subject being forced to be a patient, then the therapy should be prohibited and the therapist punished as a criminal; the claim that the 'patient' benefits from the therapy should not be accepted as a justification for subjecting him to it.

In short, in a free society, there can be no valid objection to psychotherapy between consenting adults; nor can there be any valid defense of the 'therapeutic rape' of the patient by the therapist.

Psychiatrists are fond of reproaching me for the fact that, unlike them, I offer no help, or 'refuse' to help, severely mentally ill or psychotic persons. This accusation implies that psychiatric coercion is legitimate and indeed praiseworthy — the paradigmatic claim of psychiatry that I reject. As a 'therapist' I try to help persons only if they want and seek my help; and my aim is always to try to help them become more free and responsible. Hence, I have nothing to offer persons who do not want my help or whose aim is to reject their freedom and coerce others to assume responsibility for them.

Punishment

Our prisons, called 'correctional institutions', are supposed to rehabilitate; our madhouses, called 'mental hospitals', and supposed to treat. By denying that criminals are punished and mental hospital patients stored, we obscure the nature of both criminal and psychiatric sanctions, undermining the legitimacy of punishing lawbreakers, and concealing the illegitimacy of imprisoning persons innocent of law-breaking.

There is much speculation nowadays about whether lawbreakers should be punished or treated. This problem disappears if we define punishment and treatment not in terms of the subject's condition at the end of the intervention, but his intention at the beginning of it. Punishments are interventions which the subject, called 'criminal', would avoid if he could and submits to by force; whereas treatments are interventions which the subject, called 'patient', seeks and submits to by choice. Subsequently, the result of either intervention may be judged to be helpful or harmful by the subject himself or by others. However, the outcome of punishment or treatment should not confuse us about whether the process that led to it was coerced or free.

There can be only two responses to deviance: repression or tolerance. Those who define deviance and are disturbed by it must either coerce the deviants into conformity (or kill them), or must learn to tolerate and live with them.

The current liberal psychiatric position on the death penalty is callous hypocrisy concealed as compassionate reverence for life (except for that of the unborn). Revolted by the anti-death penalty cant prominently featured in the pages of the *New York Times*, a recently released Federal prisoner writes: " . . . it [the death penalty] is much kinder than a sentence of 25 years in prison. . . . Many death-row inmates might well choose death in lieu of a mandatory 25-year sentence . . . Witness the high rate of prison suicide or attempted suicide . . . "[1]

Opponents of the death penalty don't really care about the lives or deaths of prisoners. If they did, they would want to give them a choice — between a painful life in prison and a painless release from it by death (by means of appropriate drugs put at their disposal by the prison authorities).

Crime is illegal behavior; mental illness is illegitimate behavior. Since illegal behavior is, by definition, illegitimate, it is not surprising that crime is increasingly viewed as mental illness, and that psychiatric sanctions increasingly replace criminal penalties.

RELIGION

Religion: 1. Boundless conceit concealed as utmost modesty. 2. Justification for regulating one's own behavior and coercing others to regulate theirs. 3. An inexhaustible mine of meaning for the mentally lazy.

"If there is no God, everything is permitted," said Dostoyevsky. He was only half right. Because if there is a God, everything is still permitted, the perpetrators of evil never failing to secure His blessings.

Today, two of the most important contemporary religions are communism and psychiatry. Each is based on the principle, proclaimed by their high priests, that human behavior is determined by scientific laws and that individuals have no free will. And each consists of the practice, zealously pursued by their leading practitioners, of systematically depriving individuals of the freedom to make uncoerced choices.

God neither failed nor died, but was murdered. His

killers, who have usurped His place, use as their fronts the two enterprises of the modern age whose legitimacy cannot be questioned: the State and Science. Two of His assassins are Marx and Freud, one of whom characterized religion as 'opium', the other as a 'neurosis'. In communist hands, religion freely professed thus becomes a dangerous drug that must be outlawed, while religion brutally enforced becomes Scientific Marxism which the whole world must embrace. In psychiatric hands, religion freely professed becomes an illness that must be cured, while religion brutally enforced becomes a scientific treatment to which the whole world must submit.

Students of religion call persons who insist that the Bible or the Koran are the words of God 'literalists', as in the following typical statement: "Al-Ashari [a tenth-century Islamic scholar] was a literalist . . . he accepted literaly the statements that God has hands and that he sits upon a throne . . . "[1]

Scholars who interpret religious language figuratively are invariably called 'non-fundamentalistic' or 'liberal'. This is an evasion. The opposite of a literal interpretation of a text is a metaphorical interpretation of it. In scholarly discussions of religion, however, such clarity is carefully avoided. Why? Because a metaphorical interpretation of the Bible or the Koran is, in plain English, an atheistic interpretation of it: if such sacred texts are God's words only in the same sense that the stock markets 'speak' to financial analysts, then, of course, they are not God's words at all. In which case we may be expected to respect them as sage advice, but could not be expected to revere them as holy revelation.

Academic theologians now write endless tomes on the 'deep metaphors' of religion and the mental health professions — subtly legitimizing both. At the same time, they studiously avoid discussing the practical significance of distinguishing between interpreting religious and psychiatric symbols metaphorically or literally. By ignoring literalized metaphors, they miss the tragi-comedy of life and legitimize prevailing authority. Consider, for example, the case of the evangelist Oral Roberts asking the faithful to send him eight million dollars lest "the Lord bring me home". This threat of predicting one's own demise by theological rather than secular (suicidal) means, worked on those who interpreted his message literally: To save his life, the faithful sent him eight million dollars. Interpreting Roberts's message metaphorically and replying in kind, one might have sent him a telegram with some such message as this: 'Congratulations! Now you can dine with God'; or 'Bon voyage! Remember me to His son.' Actually — even today, even in our nominally secular society — such language strikes many people as offensive and would be deemed unprintable by the editors of many newspapers and magazines.

We can say that a man is a 'son of a bitch', or a 'son of a gun', or a 'son of God'. No one interprets the first or the second phrase literally; but many so interpret the third phrase, and those who don't are disparaged (or worse) by those who do.

The American Constitutional doctrine of the separation of Church and State means simply that religion and government are free and independent of one another. But freedom is a burden as well as an opportunity: in this case, the burden is that religion must manage without the support of the government, and government without the support of religion. It is not surprising, then, that this lofty principle has been under steady attack, along two main fronts: taxation and psychiatry. By granting tax exemption to churches, the Internal Revenue Service functions, in effect, as a Federal agency, legitimizing belief systems the government recognizes as religion, and illegitimizing, as 'cults', belief systems it does not so recognize. *Mutatis mutandis*, by defining membership in a religion as a manifestation of mental health and membership in a cult as a symptom of mental illness, psychiatry functions as a quasi-federal agency legitimizing what it recognizes as a religion, and illegitimizing what it does not as a cult.

American liberals fear the 'religious right' as a threat to civil liberties. However, because of the Constitution, religions recognized as religions pose no real threat to our liberties—whereas religions masquerading as non-religions (especially psychiatry and therapy) do.

Monotheism is the worship of a God *qua* power-monopolist. Hence the idolization of the monopolistic power of *one* God, *one* Church, *one* pope, *one* sovereign — and the contradiction and conflict between monotheism and individual liberty-and-responsibility. *Mutatis mutandis*, as monopolistic religion is the worship of the one true God and system of worship, so monopolistic medicine is the worship of the one true idea of health and system of curing disease. We Americans now idealize and idolize the monopolistic alliance of Scientific Medicine and the Nation State in the same way as people in pre-Reformation Christian nations idealized and idolized the monopolistic alliance of True Faith and the State. I believe we have thus misinterpreted the nature, and overestimated the degree, of personal freedom and responsibility we have gained since the Enlightenment and through the Scientific Revolution.

The Jewish God scolds and exacts revenge. The Christian God loves and forgives. But neither laughs. The Greeks and Romans had gods that laughed. For the Jew or Christian, the very idea of divine laughter is sacrilege. Why? Because, unlike the Greek and Roman deities, the Jewish and Christian gods do not truly accept man as man. The Jew must placate God, who is forever angry and whose standards of piety leave not the tiniest crack of life uninfused by His exacting demands. The Christian must please God, who treats him as *ab origine* sinful and whom he cannot truly please so long as he lives.

Laughter, in contrast, is the ultimate expression of acceptance and approval, and solemnity (even more than scolding and punishment), the ultimate expression of disapproval and disdain. That is why comedians make us feel comfortable, and preachers uncomfortable (encouraging us, however, to feel especially worthy precisely because we feel unworthy).

Persons in positions of authority and power — particularly parents, priests, and politicians — can help others become dependent on them: that is, become obedient 'children'; or they can help them become dependent on themselves: that is, become independent adults. History teaches us that persons who make others dependent on them are worshipped, whereas those who help them become independent are disdained or ignored. So long as 'God' is loved and 'Satan' hated, there can be no liberation of the human spirit.

SCHIZOPHRENIA

If you talk to God, you are praying; if God talks to you, you have schizophrenia.

When a man says he is Jesus, he is not complaining; he is boasting. We consider his claim a symptom of illness, he considers it a stamp of greatness.

When a man says he is Jesus or makes some other claim that seems to us outrageous, we call him psychotic and lock him up in the madhouse. Freedom of speech is only for normal people.

If you believe that you are Jesus or that the Communists are after you (and they are not) — then your belief is likely to be regarded as a symptom of schizophrenia. But if you believe that Jesus is the Son of God or that Communism is the only scientifically and morally correct form of government — then your belief is likely to be regarded as a reflection of who you are: Christian or Communist. This is why I think that we will discover the chemical cause of schizo-

phrenia when we discover the chemical cause of Christianity and Communism. No sooner and no later.

Psychiatrists look for defective genes and twisted
molecules as the causes of schizophrenia, because schizophrenia is the name of a disease. If Christianity or Communism were called diseases, would psychiatrists look for
their chemical and genetic causes?

Schizophrenia 'is': 1. The cancer of conceit. 2. Early
retirement from life. 3. Being never available to anyone.
4. The psychiatrist's professionally legitimized lies about
the patient.

Schizophrenia is a declaration, not a disease. What does
the subject assert? A conceited capitulation: 'I won't struggle for the rewards the world has to offer; I refuse to lower
myself and get down into the dirt of everyday life; I am too
good for that.'

When it was invented in 1911, schizophrenia was said
to be incurable. Since then, it has allegedly been cured with
insulin coma, metrazol shock, electric shock, lobotomy,
and neuroleptic drugs. In 1988, still another cure was announced: the transplantation of embryonic brain tissue into
the brain of the schizophrenic patient.[1] This emperor, as I

have remarked elsewhere, has so many beautiful robes that it is unthinkable that he should not exist.[2]

Schizophrenia, psychiatrists maintain, is a 'thought disturbance'. By the same token one could say that heresy is a 'belief disturbance'. In each case, the question is: Who is 'disturbed'? If the subject himself, he is free to seek relief for his disturbance. If others, disturbed by the schizophrenic/heretic, they are free to seek relief for their disturbance. My aim with respect to the political and social situation of the schizophrenic (mental patient) has simply been to extend to him the same protection from psychiatric persecution which is guaranteed to the heretic (religious dissenter or deviant) from religious persecution.

"The real object of the [First] amendment," declared Justice Joseph Story, "was not to countenance, much less advance, Mahometanism, or Judaism, or infidelity . . . but to exclude all rivalry among Christian sects. . . . It thus cuts off the means of religious persecution (the vice and pest of former ages) and of the subversion of the rights of conscience in matters of religion . . . "[3]

Similarly, the object of extending the protections of the First Amendment to beliefs now categorized as psychiatric is not to countenance, much less advance, 'crazy' or 'delusional' beliefs, but to exclude all rivalry, with respect to what constitutes 'rationality', among religious, psychiatric, and other systems of beliefs. This would cut off the means of psychiatric persecution (the vice and pest of the Age of

Reason) and of the subversion of the rights of conscience in matters of psychiatry . . .

From testimony given at the trial of John W. Hinckley, Jr.:

William T. Carpenter, Professor of Psychiatry at the University of Maryland: "[Hinckley suffers from] process schizophrenia"[4] (June 7, 1982).

Park E. Dietz, M.D., Professor of Psychiatry at the University of Virginia: "Hinckley does not suffer from schizophrenia"[4] (June 7, 1982).

David M. Bear, Assistant Professor of Psychiatry at Harvard Medical School: "[CAT scans] were absolutely essential [to my diagnosis of schizophrenia]"[4] (May 21, 1982).

David Davis, M.D., Professor of Radiology at George Washington University Medical Center: "There is no possible way that you can predict people's behavior, or whether they are schizophrenic or not schizophrenic, from a CAT scan, period"[4] (June 3, 1982).

The lover and the schizophrenic display opposite dispositions: the lover is attached, intimate, passionate, and longs (for the Other); whereas the schizophrenic is detached, lonely, aloof, and is uninterested (in the Other). This is consistent with the fact that 'everyone loves a lover'

and we consider such a person to be especially fortunate; whereas everyone hates a schizophrenic and we consider such a person to be especially unfortunate.

Some schizophrenic speech is simply a form of idle chatter. Clearly, the patient does not take his own utterances seriously. He merely makes noise, perhaps to distract himself. From what? His insignificance? Shallowness? Helplessness? The realization that no one is listening and that, in any case, he has nothing to say that is worth listening to?

The person displaying the symptoms of schizophrenia pretends that he is not an agent: he acts as if he were an object. Similarly, the psychiatrist diagnosing a person as a schizophrenic pretends that the patient is not an agent: he treats him as if he were an object.

The so-called schizophrenic is often a person who refuses to admit that he has lived badly, is useless, guilty, or sinful. He rids himself of his bad conscience by projecting it, hence the accusing voices he hears. Only the truth, as Jesus admonished, can set him free. But what if he does not want to be set free because he prefers that others take care of him as a psychiatric invalid? The more clearly we understand schizophrenia in moral terms, the more absurd it is to speak of *treating* persons so *diagnosed.*

Consider the following terms:

TYPHOID FEVER

SPRING FEVER

Typhoid fever is an infectious, febrile disease caused by the typhoid bacillus.

Spring fever is not an illness, does not cause fever, and has no medically meaningful cause. Webster's defines it as; "*Humorous.* The lazy listless feeling that comes to persons with the first warm days of spring."

Perhaps some day dictionaries will define schizophrenia as follows: "*Obsolete.* A term formerly used to disguise the medical misinterpretation of the lazy, listless feeling, especially of adolescents and young adults, that comes over them with the first realization that they must stand on their own feet."

If your circulation fails, you have ischemia. If your kidneys fail, you have uremia. If your life fails, you have schizophrenia.

To cure ischemia, doctors transplant blood vessels. To cure uremia, they transplant kidneys. What should they transplant to cure schizophrenia?

If our life were an organ, it might be possible for doctors to repair its malfunctioning, perhaps by replacing it with another. But our life is not a part of us, it is us. That is why no one else can fix it when it malfunctions, or replace it when it fails.

According to AMI (the Alliance for the Mentally Ill of New York State), schizophrenia is "a pervasive brain disorder which appears to have a genetic basis." Seemingly in support of this contention, the newsletter of AMI next notes "that the course of the disease . . . is better in Nigerian and Indian villages than in New York or European cities."[5] I dare say this assertion is not true for any *real* disease.

Different observers may *call* the same person a religious fanatic, a victim of political persecution, or a paranoid schizophrenic. Each of these categories implies a mixture of description and judgment, in much the same way as does *calling* the same glass half-full or half-empty. If we want to assemble an adequate sample of, say, eight-ounce glasses containing four ounces of liquid, we must do so by ascertaining that the volume of liquid in each is exactly one-half its total capacity, not by what people call them. Thus, we cannot study schizophrenia biologically unless we assemble our sample of 'schizophrenics' according to some objective criterion. Actually, what now counts as schizophrenia is what 'consensus groups' composed of prestigious psychiatrists choose to *call* schizophrenia, much as what counts as a miracle is what 'consensus groups' composed of prestigious priests choose to *call* a miracle. This may satisfy the faithful, but carries no weight with the skeptic.

As psychiatric doctrine has it, the typical schizophrenic

patient begins to manifest symptoms of his illness during late adolescence; nevertheless, he often lives to a ripe old age in robust health, without evidence of neurological or psychological deterioration, even in the seventh or eighth decade of his life. If schizophrenia is a brain disease, that is, plainly, a remarkable course for it to follow.

The natural history of schizophrenia has engendered skepticism toward it in some psychiatrists, but not many; few share the sentiments ably articulated by Myre Sim:

> For most of this century, on the basis of the most authoritative laboratory evidence of the time, schizophrenia has been variously attributed to degeneration of the interstitial cells of the testes, degeneration of the liver, and malfunctions of the kidneys, adrenals, and thyroid. The frontal lobes have also been implicated as have vitamin deficiencies and a variety of metabolic disorders. Yet, schizophrenics had the longest expectations of life among residents of mental hospitals and they enjoyed such rude health that they constituted the greatest security risk. You may be excused if you have concluded that all this laboratory work was done by second or third raters. Far from it. The man who provided 'proof' of the testicular degeneration theory was elected a Fellow of the Royal Society of London and was later knighted."[6]

With increasing zeal psychiatrists assert that schizophenia is a brain disease. Let us assume that 'it' is. (The quotation marks are intended to alert the reader to the problematic character of what 'it' is.) Would that help us cope with the 'problems of schizophrenia'? Or would it instead help us see more clearly that the belief that schizophenia is a brain disease conceals moral and social problems not susceptible to solution by medical research or treatment?

Suppose that a person neglects his health and hygiene, perhaps even speaks about killing himself, 'because' he suffers from schizophrenia. Would that still justify incarcerating him in a mental hospital against his will? Or that he killed his wife and children, or shot the President, 'because' he suffered from schizophrenia. Would that still justify excusing his criminal behavior and incarcerating him in a mental hospital against his will?

I believe that the identification of brain disorders correlatable with behavioral deviations (assuming such correlations exist for what are now called mental illnesses) would increase, rather than diminish, our commonsense disposition to treat our fellow man as a responsible and respectable moral agent—deserving of human rights if he obeys the law, and of humane punishment if he does not.

In the United States today, a person has the right to refuse to give blood for an AIDS test; hence, he can, in effect, prevent others from diagnosing him as having AIDS.

There is, of course, no blood test (or any other physical or chemical test) for schizophrenia. Giving or refusing permission for a blood test is thus irrelevant for a diagnosis of schizophrenia; hence, a person cannot prevent others from diagnosing him as having schizophrenia.

Suppose, then, that the dreams of biological psychiatrists were realized and schizophrenia were a biological disease diagnosable by means of a blood test. Would a person suspected of having schizophrenia have the right to refuse giving blood for a test for it and hence, in effect, refuse to be diagnosed as having schizophrenia?

The supreme irony about professional and popular reports concerning schizophrenia is that they invariably take for granted that, in order to cope effectively with the alleged disease, scientists must, first of all, discover its etiology. But this is simply not true. Indeed, from a practical (legal, political, social) point of view, it is relatively unimportant what (if anything) causes schizophrenia.

Inevitably, physicians (and people generally) are more interested in controlling some diseases and patients than others. For example, AIDS and arthritis are both diseases with clearly demonstrable bodily manifestations and somatic causes; but we are more eager to control patients with AIDS than patients with arthritis. So long as psychiatrists (and jurists and people generally) attribute homicide and suicide and other disturbing behaviors to schizophrenia, we will want to control patients suffering from it regardless of its cause.

The idea of insanity as an 'alien power' lurking 'out there' ever ready to enslave and oppress us — exemplified by schizophrenia — supports psychiatry as an ideological theory and movement of liberation.[7] The fact that schizophrenia is a fiction and those posturing as our would-be liberators from it are the problem rather than the solution has not impaired the credibility of the mental health movement any more than have similar failings impaired the credibility of other modern liberation movements. The human dread of disorder is evidently so powerful that it obliterates, in every generation, the memory of what ideological liberators have wrought throughout history; indeed, it obliterates even the obvious reality of the present, denying or falsifying what modern man has done to man in the name of diagnosing and treating schizophrenia.

SEX

A glossary:

Infatuation: The name an observer gives to the condition of a man intensely attracted to a woman (or vice versa) when, according to the observer, the only thing the couple have in common is their sexual difference.

Masturbation: 1. Taking matters into one's own hands; which is why authorities either prohibit or prescribe it (in an effort to maintain control over the individual). 2. The primary sexual activity of mankind: in the nineteenth century, a disease; in the twentieth, a cure.

Perversion: Sexual practice disapproved of by the speaker.

Sex therapist: Pimp and procurer with clinical credentials.

Love: The desire to merge lives — yielding, at best, companionship.

Lust: The desire to merge bodies—yielding, at best, copulation.

Marriage: 1. The desire to merge both bodies and lives—yielding, as a rule, the sacrifice of copulation for companionship or vice versa. 2. The state or condition of a community consisting of a husband, a wife, and two victims, making in all two.[7]

Formerly, young persons who engaged in sexual acts were called 'promiscuous'; now they are called 'sexually active'. As this example illustrates, it is virtually impossible to speak about sexual conduct without blaming or praising it. The same is true, of course, of all human behavior that really matters.

One can teach a person to eat dietetically proper meals, but one cannot teach him to be a gourmet. Similarly, one can teach a person to perform sexually, but one cannot teach him to be erotic.

Pornography is to sex as vulgarity is to language.

There are two sexes. They could be called 'complementary' but are called 'opposites'. Is this not more revealing of the true relations between the sexes than the whole lexicon of love?

One of the most powerful aphrodisiacs is the anticipation of erotic embrace with an absent beloved. It combines affection, lust, and novelty with the promise of fulfillment. The pleasurable exhilaration so generated is the very opposite of the dull and distasteful sensation of obligation engendered by the unremitting presence and availability of the partner, however beloved and sexually attractive.

Traditionally, men used power to gain sex, and women sex to gain power. The new ethic of equality between men and women must come down to one of two things: either, as the romantics hope, that neither men nor women will use power to gain sex; or, as the realists expect, that both men and women will use power to gain sex, and sex to gain power.

Why is the sexual arousal and release of women more interesting (even for women) than the arousal and release of men? Because the process is visually not so obvious, leaving more to the imagination, which is the ultimate source of sexual curiosity. This should tell people something about the connection between sex and secrecy, but they do not want to hear what it is.

One cannot be an individual, a person separate from others (family, society, and so forth), without having secrets. It is because secrets separate people that individualists treasure them and collectivists condemn them. As keeping secrets separates people, so sharing them brings them together. Gossip, confessional, psychoanalysis, each involves communicating secrets and thus establishing human relationships. Traditionally, sex has been a very private, secretive activity. Herein perhaps lies its power for uniting people in a strong bond. As we make sex less secretive, we may rob it of its power to hold men and women together.

Orgasm is the quintessential paradox and, perhaps because of it, the quintessential pleasure in the entire range of human experience. This is because orgasm is the controlled experience of loss of control. If the loss of control over sexual arousal and response is overcontrolled, or if the control under which the loss is experienced is inadequate, the orgastic experience is impaired or absent. Conversely, the more unrestrained is the loss of control and the more secure the control under which it is lost, the greater is the intensity of the orgastic experience. In short, the pleasure of genital orgasm is the consequence of a well-articulated experience of controlled loss of control. This is why, in human societies, sex is both a brutalizing and a civilizing force.

Sexual desire may be a powerful impetus for bonding in animals but is an enormous barrier to comfortable relations among human beings. The reason is that sexual desire is rarely exactly reciprocal between two persons: as a rule, either the man lusts more passionately after the woman than she does for him, or vice versa. But in the end, no one wants to lust after an unwilling, or even less willing, partner; nor does anyone want to be lusted after, and be the 'sex object' of, a more lusting partner. This may be the main reason why sexual attraction and desire cannot serve as the foundation for marriage or lasting friendship.

SOCIAL RELATIONS

A person cannot make another happy, but he can make him unhappy. This is the main reason why there is more unhappiness than happiness in the world.

The truth shall set us free, said Jesus. But it is lies that unite us.

Mysticism joins and unites; reason divides and separates. People crave belonging more than understanding. Hence the prominent role of mysticism, and the limited role of reason, in human affairs.

The two principal monomanias of modern man: Monotheism and monogamy.

Two wrongs don't make a right, but they make a good excuse.

When a person can no longer laugh at himself, it is time for others to laugh at him.

The adage 'Crime does not pay' is false; if it were true, there would be no crime.

If you have strongly held opinions, you are opinionated; if you don't, you lack conviction: either way, there is something wrong with you.

Impertinence: The name authorities give to the aspirations for, and declarations of, independence of their inferiors.

In Karl Marx's and Sigmund Freud's vision, man is victim of oppression or repression; in Adam Smith's and Ludwig von Mises's vision, man is a victor over instinct and impulse. The former vision supports the collectivist-totalitarian dream of liberating man from the slavery of brutal capitalists and harsh superegos. The latter supports the individualist-libertarian dream of man controlling his own impulses and peacefully co-operating with like-minded others.

Equality in human relations is like the ideal gas in physics. The most we can expect in real life is mutually satisfying reciprocity (which, ironically, is hindered rather than hastened by strivings for equality).

It is fashionable nowadays to assert, in the manner of Kant, that if one person 'uses' another, the true humanity of both is violated; and hence that, in a morally proper relationship, a person should not use another. This is idealistic humbug. People always use each other. Human relationships are good or bad, moral or immoral, depending not on whether people use each other, but on how they do so.

The natural state of mankind is poverty; wealth is something man must create. Similarly, the natural state of mankind is 'mental illness' (in the sense of being undisciplined, useless, and infantile); 'mental health' (in the sense of being competent, self-responsible, and caring for one's family) is something man must create. It is therefore wrong to think of poverty or mental illness as being 'caused', but it is right to think of wealth and mental health in that way: this is why poverty and mental illness must be overcome by the personal effort of the affected individual — while a person may lose his wealth and mental health without his participation or even against his will. Moreover, just as no amount of religion and prayer can transform an undisciplined and uneducated peasant into an effective farmer producing a surplus of food, so no amount of psychiatry and anti-psychotic drugs can transform an undisciplined and uneducated youth into an effective person producing marketable goods or services.

In close personal relationships, people often either envy
or pity one another.

Power and powerlessness both corrupt. The more widely power is diffused among people, the more dignified will
be the relationship among them.

Paternalism is a mortal enemy of dignity: How can a
person feel dignified *vis-à-vis* a medical profession, a
judiciary, a government that never says to him: 'I don't
know. It's none of my business. It's your problem. You deal
with it.'

It is misleading to speak of phenomena such as slavery
or involuntary mental hospitalization as 'social problems'
since they are, in fact, arrangements representing solutions
that people have evolved and adopted to solve certain other
problems, for example, the need for cheap human labor or
for controlling certain troublesome members of society.
Calling such solutions 'problems' implies that people are
eager and willing to eschew the benefits they derive from
them, which is usually not true. Once it becomes true, the
arrangement ceases to be an acceptable solution and is
quickly abandoned. Such was the case, for example, with
the practice of confining Japanese-Americans in so-called
relocation camps, which stopped as soon as World War II
ended. The fact that coercive psychiatric practices have
become a chronic social problem thus suggests that it is not
a problem that people are trying to solve, but rather

a manifestation of our intense ambivalence about insane behavior and psychiatric coercion.

Great jurists are made by sacrificing plaintiffs to the Constitution; great physicians, by sacrificing patients to Research. The moral: if you value your freedom and health, don't be a test case in the court or the clinic.

What is a friend? For some, a sycophant; for others, an incorruptible but loving critic.

Beware of feeling sorry for someone who can harm you. It is a luxury only the very powerful or very masochistic can afford.

If you feel sorry for yourself, someone will soon give you something to be sorry about.

Articulate persons argue. Inarticulate persons quarrel.

Beware of the person who treats you as if he had no obligations to you: Like a rapist, he will reduce you to an object of his desires — to satisfy his lust for self-gratification.

Beware of the person who treats you as if you had no obligations to him: Like a therapist, he will reduce you to an object of his duties — to satisfy his lust for self-esteem.

Beware of the person who never says 'I am sorry'. He is weak and frightened and will, sometimes at the slightest provocation, fight with the desperate ferocity of a cornered animal.

Suttee (also sati): 1. The Indian/Hindu custom of a wife placing herself (or being forced to place herself) on her dead husband's funeral pyre. 2. A sacred ritual, suicide, or murder, depending on circumstances and the observer's viewpoint. 3. Autopyromania, a fatal mental illness not yet recognized by the science of psychiatry that knows no national boundaries.

How men hate waiting, for a few hours, while their wives shop for clothes and trinkets; how women hate waiting, often for much of their lives, while their husbands shop for fame and glory.

Insofar as motherhood is an occupation, it is reasonable to ask the same questions about it that one might ask about any other, namely: how many members of this particular occupational class does society need? How many is it able or willing to support?

We appear unable or willing to accept the reality of human conflict. It is never simply man who offends against his fellow man: someone or something — the Devil, mental illness — intervenes, to obscure, excuse, and explain away man's terrifying inhumanity to man.

There are two kinds of leadership — for dependence and independence. Historically, the only readily recognizable kind has been leadership for dependence. When successful, it results in the recruitment of faithful followers who, through their claims and conduct, confirm the glory and validate the wisdom of the Great Leader.

In contrast, leadership for independence is of low visibility and hence difficult to recognize. When successful, it results in independent individuals who, through their claims and conduct, confirm only their own authenticity.

Being the master *in* a system is not the same as being the master *of* it. Indeed, to be dominant in an autocratic system is to be dominated by it as well: the slave is ruled by the iron fist, the master by the hand in the velvet glove.

People can stand each other only for a limited period — hence they protect themselves either by ceremonial distancing or by physical escape. Insular societies with limited space, such as Japan, exemplify the former; continental societies with seemingly unlimited space, such as the United States, the latter.

In Japan, social conflict is managed, as a rule, by ceremonial separation: wife is kept at a distance from husband, worker from manager, and generally, subordinate from superior, not by physical distance, but by social distancing. This requires establishing discrete existential spaces for the contestants.

In the United States, social conflict is managed, as a rule, by physical separation: the Indian is exiled to the reservation, the young man goes West, husband and wife divorce, the mentally ill are segregated. This requires establishing discrete geographical spaces for the contestants.

In science, it's dangerous to lie: if discovered, the liar is cast out of the group as a faker and fraud.

In religion, politics, and psychiatry, it's dangerous to tell the truth: if discovered, the truth-teller is cast out of the group as a heretic and a traitor.

Our biological existence begins in the womb and our social existence in society, and, more narrowly, in the family. Over these beginnings we, ourselves, have no control whatever. Our complete passivity — our inability to have or exercise our intention or will — does not last long, however. Soon, we are expected to eat and sleep only at certain times. Next, we are expected to control the functioning of our bladder and bowel, and then all of our musculature.

As social beings, we thus begin our lives with responsibilities: childhood is a period of tutelage during which (as a rule) we are given many responsibilities, but acquire or have few rights. This important disjunction between responsibilities and rights is repeated, most glaringly in the institution of slavery, and, less obviously but just as importantly, in the relations between superiors and inferiors in religion, medicine, and the countless paternalistic arrangements through which human beings seek to reinstitute the original parent-child relationship.

The error in attributing human behavior to drives, instincts, mental (brain) diseases, or other impersonal (non-willed) elements is that *all* human behavior is learned. By which I mean simply that although *what* we do may be biologically driven, *when, where,* and *how* we do it is learned. Eating, drinking, urinating, and so forth are biologically driven; but we learn when, where, and how to eat, drink, urinate, and so forth.

Accordingly, we could view nearly everything we do as learning, performing, or teaching *how* to do X — where X may stand for playing chess or tennis, speaking or writing, helping or harming, obeying the law or breaking it, and so forth; in short, where X may stand for *how to live* (as we ourselves expect and want to live, or as others expect and want us to live, or some combination of both).

All modern ideologies view certain classes of persons (or even all persons) as *victims* suffering from *oppression*, and promise them *liberation*. For example, in communism, the oppressed are the workers, the oppressors the capitalists; in feminism, they are the women and the men; and in psychiatry/psychoanalysis, the oppressed are all of mankind, enslaved by their mental illness or unconscious. Accordingly, the adherents of these belief systems seek salvation in liberation from their oppressors. But what happens when they achieve liberation, either by their own efforts, or, as has happened more often in the twentieth century, because their oppressors withdraw from the scene? What typically happens is that the formerly oppressed claim non-responsibility for their inability to care or provide for themselves and demand that others (their own State or other States) take care of them.

At home, we see women, granted equal rights with men, rejecting responsibility for the consequences of their behavior and demanding that others (the taxpayer) pay for their abortions or for caring for their children. Similarly, we see mental patients, occasionally granted their liberty, clamoring that others (the taxpayers) pay for their shelter or for a 'therapy' fully under their own control. Abroad, we see formerly colonial people, granted political independence, rejecting responsibility for the consequences of their behavior and demanding that others (especially Americans) feed their growing populations. Paradoxically, in each of these cases, we strongly approve of recognizing such people's right to liberty, but equally strongly disap-

prove of treating them as fully responsible for their actions
and for the consequences of their actions.

The doctrinal beliefs of biological psychiatry and
feminism are the two favorite shibboleths of late twentieth-
century America. According to the first, mental illnesses
are biological abnormalities that justify psychiatric coercions; according to the second, there are no biological differences between men and women significant enough to
justify legal, political, or social distinctions between the
sexes. The former *affirms* a biological basis for problems in
living; the latter *denies* a biological basis for existential differences between men and women. Each of these falsehoods
is now acclaimed as Official Truth: The person who rejects
the prevailing psychiatric orthodoxy is 'denying the reality
of mental illness'; whereas the person who rejects the
prevailing feminist orthodoxy is 'advocating sex discrimina-
tion'.

Persons whose lives are dull and insignificant look for
significance in the past or the future. This is why a glo-
rified, mythologized religious, racial, or national past is so
important for some people; and why the glorious, utopian
future of one's children, party, nation, or even all of
mankind, fore-ordained by salvational religion or politics,
is so important for others.

Life is a joke God plays on us. Some take the joke too

seriously: they are likely to become fanatics or madmen. Others don't take it seriously enough: they are likely to become humorists or libertarians. Most people, of course, take it just the right way: they are likely to become normal persons.

SUICIDE

Suicide: The only (literal) escape from a life sentence. (Death by accident or illness is not willed and hence doesn't count.)

We now view suicide as a disease: hence the efforts to 'prevent' and 'treat' it. But suicide is more like a treatment: it is the only effective remedy against what sometimes ails people — namely, the necessity to go on living.

As they grow up, children learn to what extent they are allowed and expected to take their lives in their own hands. The more they are and do so, the more likely they are to develop into autonomous, self-determining persons — who not only take their lives in their own hands, but who also take their own lives. This is why those who choose to be their own masters often also choose to be their own executioners.

The person who engages in behavior psychiatrists call a 'suicidal gesture' or a 'suicidal threat' offends not because he (allegedly) wants to die, which is his inalienable right, but because he involves the public in what ought to be a private act. His offense, in short, is similar to that of the exhibitionist.

Every man has an inalienable right to his penis, but no man has a right to exhibit it in public. Similarly, every man has an inalienable right to his intention to kill himself, but no man has the right to impose it on the public. The person who exhibits his intention to kill himself is indiscreet and indecorous, not insane.

In the ideology and jargon of psychiatry-and-law, a severely mentally ill person is considered to be, *ipso facto*, 'dangerous to himself and others'. Like the metaphor of mental illness, this nonsensical phrase is used to justify involuntary psychiatric incarceration and 'treatment' and is thus pivotal to the psychiatric enterprise.

While it makes sense to say that a person is dangerous to others, it makes no sense to say that he is dangerous to himself (unless we assume, *a priori*, that he has two selves, one sane and another insane, the latter being dangerous to the former). But the person who wants to die differs from the person who wants to get rich only in his goal. Either or both of these persons might be said to be 'dangerous to himself', the phrase simply disguising that the speaker considers the actor's motives illegitimate.

Suicide is to homocide as masturbation is to rape. Perhaps if killing oneself were called 'auto-homicide', and killing others 'hetero-homicide', the distinction between these acts would be more precise and our understanding of them more profound.

Living well requires careful planning and unrelenting vigilance in making decisions. Since dying is part of living, how can we expect dying well to require anything less? To be sure, the phrase *dying well*, like the phrase *living well*, has no more meaning than we give it and we must be candid, especially with ourselves, about what we intend it to mean. To persons who value the *vita activa*, living well — besides being the best revenge — means being self-determining and self-reliant. Both childhood and old age are, in such a view, disabilities, because they entail a diminution of our capacity for independent, self-directed action. It follows that if living well is contingent on planning, choice, and self-determination, so must dying well be; and if the paradigm of the former attitude is the use of birth control by those engaged in (non-procreative) sexual intercourse, then the paradigm of the latter attitude must be death control ('suicide') by those contemplating (non-passive) dying.

We call dying by disease 'natural death', and dying by choice 'suicide'. Although in our political language we celebrate the value of autonomy, in our medical language we celebrate the value of heteronomy. If we valued (medical) self-responsibility more, and dependence (on medical authority) less, we would call drug abuse 'self-medication' and suicide 'self-determined death'.

Countless people today preach the virtue of individual liberty and responsibility, but few practice it. For example, mental health professionals typically see themselves as trying to liberate their patients from being the slaves of their past and help them become the masters of their future. But they don't mean it: they pretend that a person could become the executor of his own life without also becoming his own potential executioner. The psychiatric prohibition of suicide today, like the psychiatric prohibition of masturbation which it displaced, is emblematic of the community's hostility to autonomy and of the mental health professional's role as agent of social conformity.

Today, if a person says — especially to a mental health professional — 'I am going to kill myself', the listener takes it for granted that it is his moral and professional duty to try to prevent the speaker from killing himself. This is, *prima facie,* a very odd way to respond to such a statement.

Suppose a person were to say: 'I will start smoking two packs of cigarettes a day . . .'; or 'I will go on a diet of egg yolks, ice cream, and french fries . . .'; or 'I will go shopping and spend more money than I can afford . . .'; or any other similar statement implying that he will embark on self-injurious behavior that may, sooner or later, harm or kill him. Would we feel it is our duty to talk him out of doing so? To treat him for a mental illness? To forcibly restrain him in order to prevent his carrying out the promised action? If the answer is no with respect to smoking, overeating, and overspending, why is it, why should it be, yes with respect to suicide?

If Jones doesn't want to stay married, or live in the United States, or do any number of other things—we do not consider it to be Smith's business, much less his duty, to try to keep Jones to stay married, or live in America. If, then, Jones doesn't want to go on living, why should it be Smith's business to keep him alive? What is there about being a physician (especially a psychiatrist) that gives him the right, much less the duty, to prevent a 'suicidal person' from killing himself?

Like marriage or being an American, life is a privilege, an opportunity, and a burden—in various proportions at various times, but always in the eyes of the beholder. Our current customs, laws, and psychiatric practices with respect to suicide and suicide prevention reflect not our respect for life (as we like to pretend), but merely our fear of death.

During the past century, many persons in so-called developed countries concluded that when it comes to having children, less is more; that having, say, five children was better than having ten, and having two, one, or even none better still. If we want to continue to improve our lot on Earth, we will have to apply this criterion to the length of our own life. Why should living, say, ten more years at age 70 be better than living only five, two, one, or no more years? In short, we have learned that to prosper as young adults, we must practice birth control; to prosper as aging or disabled persons, we shall have to learn to practice death control, that is, suicide.

By definition, suicide is a type of homicide — that is, the killing of a human being. Significantly, the killing of another person is recognized to be a morally and psychologically complex phenomenon: the law distinguishes among first-degree murder, second-degree murder, voluntary manslaughter, involuntary manslaughter, homicide in self-defense, and so forth. But the law recognizes only two kinds of killings of the self: namely, suicide committed while sane and suicide committed while insane (which the law regards as not suicide but accident).

Suicide is a fundamental human right. This does not mean that is it morally desirable. It means only that society does not have the moral right to interfere, by force, with a person's decision to commit this act.

If we want to enlarge the scope of personal choice and responsibility, we might assert that a person has a moral right to commit suicide or that it is a moral wrong to use the power of the state to restrain him from committing suicide. Both assertions come to the same thing, namely, denying moral legitimacy to currently fashionable coercive methods of suicide prevention.

To prohibit what one cannot enforce is to degrade both authority and obedience, thus undermining respect for both law and decency. To prohibit suicide is thus the ultimate folly, and the ultimate indecency.

He who does not accept and respect the choice to reject life does not truly accept and respect life itself.

To be accountable or responsible for preventing his patient's suicide, the psychiatrist would have to wield far-reaching powers over the patient's capacity to act. Since, in practice, it is virtually impossible to prevent the suicide of a person determined on killing himself, and since involuntary interventions to prevent suicide deprive the patient of liberty and dignity, the use of psychiatric coercion to prevent suicide is at once impractical and immoral.

On the radio and television, in books, magazines, and newspapers, we are incessantly shown and told how to kill others, but are never shown or told how to kill ourselves. Clearly, we are attracted to homicide and love to hear how to do it, but are repelled by suicide and don't want to hear how to do it. What this tells us about ourselves I leave to the reader to decide.

So massive and mindless now is the fear of suicide, especially among physicians, that sometimes they endorse euthanasia—justifying killing their 'hopelessly ill' patients with the rationalization that 'if we don't help them to die, they will kill themselves.'

In September, 1987, the delegates of the California Bar Association "approved legislation that would allow physicians to give terminally ill patients a prescription for a legal dose of drugs . . . [supporting] legislation to allow such 'doctor-assisted' suicide . . . Under the proposal, two doctors would first have to agree that the patient was certain to die within six months. A psychiatrist would have to certify that the patient was rational, and the patient's request would have to be made in writing and renewed after a 10-day waiting period."[1]

In the Age of Faith, the Church and its clerical delegates held the keys to the Kingdom of Heaven. Today, in the Age of Therapy, Medicine and its professional delegates hold the keys to the Kingdom of Death. The elemental human cry seems to be: 'Give me parents, give me priests, give me doctors, give me any authority, but don't give me autonomy — and don't leave me alone!'

In language and logic we are the prisoners of our premises, just as in politics and law we are the prisoners of our rulers. Hence we had better pick them well. For if suicide is an illness because it terminates in death and if the prevention of death by any means necessary is the physician's therapeutic mandate, then the proper remedy for suicide is indeed liberticide.

THERAPEUTIC STATE

In a Theological State it is taken for granted that the human body (like everything else) belongs to God, and that people must not tamper with it. Hence the passivist priestly attitude toward disease, exemplified by the Christian prohibition against the dissection of dead bodies.

In the Therapeutic State it is taken for granted that the human body belongs to the state (and its medical agents) and that, in the name of treatment (defined by physicians and politicians), doctors may do anything necessary to it. Hence the activist medical attitude toward disease, exemplified by the state-mandated involuntary treatment of non-existent diseases.

In a Theological State people are preoccupied with religion, salvation, and heresy; in a Therapeutic State, with health, treatment, and quackery. When religion and the state are separate, as in the United States, heresy loses its political-legal significance — and becomes a parochial issue for a particular sect, its officials and members. Similarly, were medicine and the state separate, quackery would lose its political-legal significance — and would become a parochial issue for a particular system of healing, its practitioners and followers. The absurdity of the latter prospect is a symptom of the intensity of our reliance on the state for the protection of our bodies — a dependence analogous to our ancestors' dependence on the church for the protection of their souls.

"I regard relationship addiction as a definable, diagnosable and treatable *disease process*," declares Robin Norwood, a psychotherapist and author of the 1985 best seller, *Women Who Love Too Much*.[1] Drug addiction, alcohol addiction, tobacco addiction, sex addiction, relationship addiction — diseases, one and all. Surely, we are in the grips of a medical fundamentalism no less bizarre or extreme than the religious fundamentalism of the Iranians. Ironically, we belittle the behavior of religious fundamentalists as irrational, when in fact they recognize their behavior for what it is: religious fundamentalism; whereas we deny that our behavior is a species of fundamentalism and insist that it is science blended with compassion.

Missionary clerics define natives as 'heathen', the better to be able to save them. Missionary clinicians define people as 'patients', the better to be able to cure them.

The concept of 'treatment' is the grand legitimizer of our age. Call whatever you want to do 'treatment', and, pronto, you are hailed as a great humanitarian and scientist. Freud decided to listen and talk to people, so he called conversation 'therapy' — and psychoanalysis is now recognized as a form of medical treatment. Cerletti decided to give people electrical convulsions, so he called passing an electric current through the brain 'therapy' — and electroshock is now recognized as a form of medical treatment. Masters decided to train men to perform sexually, so he called procuring prostitutes for them 'therapy' — and pimping became a form of medical treatment.

Birth and death, the two most natural and normal biological occurrences, have become pre-empted by the medical profession. Thus, pregnancy and senility are regarded as diseases whose management requires expert medical assistance. It is small wonder that the medical profession tyrannizes over the everyday life of a people who refuse to take responsibility for the most elementary tasks their biological makeup poses for them.

For the truly pious Jew (the Hasid), God and religious rules permeate all of life, leaving no behavior exempt from religious scrutiny and the proper observance of religious rules. Our present (American) world view is a kind of medical Hasidism, Health and medical rules permeating all of life, leaving no behavior exempt from medical scrutiny and the proper observance of medical rules.

In 1966, an international team of public health physicians declared that the task of the medical profession "is to bring about a change in day-to-day behavior, to create a new style of life, and almost, if we dared, *a new morality*. The aims of such an education would include sound child-rearing practices, a balanced life style, rational dietary habits, the elimination or reduction of the consumption of certain modern toxic substances such as tobacco or alcohol . . . " (emphasis added).[2]

I submit that all that the Founding Fathers sought to achieve by separating Church and State has been undone by the apostles of modern medicine whose zeal for creating a Therapeutic State has remained utterly unopposed by politicians, priests, professionals, journalists, civil libertarians, and people generally.

In a capitalist society a person can (ought to be able to) obtain narcotics in exchange for money; in a therapeutic society, he can obtain narcotics only in exchange for pain (and perhaps not even then). Capitalism generates the production of goods and services; therapeutism, the production of diseases and treatments.

In a therapeutic society, medical services are free, but people are not; in an open society, people are free, but nothing else is.

When people—especially physicians and politicians—assert that a person's life is worth *less* than he says it is, we conclude that he is a victim of oppression. Why? Because we take it for granted that no matter how worthless a person's life might seem to others, he has a right to live it as if it had value for him. Accordingly, we regard the state as despotic and despicable if it values a person's life *less* than that person himself values it and if it uses such devaluation as justification for coercing or killing the devalued individual.

On the other hand, when people — especially physicians and politicians — assert that a person's life is worth *more* than he says it is, we often conclude that he is a victim of mental illness. Why? Because we take it for granted that no matter how worthless a person's life might seem to him, he has no right to act as if it had no value to others. Accordingly, we regard the state as compassionate and therapeutic if it values a person's life *more* than that person values it himself and if it uses such overvaluation as justification for coercing the overvalued individual.

This is a terrible folly. From the point of view of the individual coerced by the state, it matters not whether the coercers justify their action with the rhetoric of undervaluing or overvaluing his life. The result is the same abrogation of personal autonomy: The individual is deprived, by the state, of his right to dispose of his mind, body, person, property, liberty, or life as he sees fit.

Conservatives want to make people virtuous; liberals want to make them healthy. Both believe that using the state to accomplish their aim is legitimate. That is why both conservatives and liberals favor anti-drug laws, psychiatric coercions, and other assaults against individual freedom and responsibility couched in therapeutic terms.

The strategy of using autocratic medical (public health

and psychiatric) controls in lieu of democratic political controls needs no longer to be inferred from the behavior of politicians: they now proudly proclaim it. Referring to David Axelrod, New York State's Health Commissioner, Governor Mario Cuomo declared: " 'Values—what basic values should this society hold—that's the key here. . . . The only difference [between Axelrod and Cuomo] is he was taught them [values] in Hebrew and maybe a little Yiddish. I was taught them in Italian and maybe a little English.' The two men [explains the reporter for the *Times*] share the same view of government—a belief that one of its chief roles is to help those who cannot help themselves. And they share the same view of government service—that it is not just a job but a kind of religious duty . . . "[3] Surely, this view of government is a far cry from that held by Locke, Burke, Jefferson, or Madison, but is very much the same cry we have heard from Rousseau, Robespierre, Lenin, and Stalin.

Two hundred years ago, the government of the United States was established on the principle that there are certain things it *must not do* to the people: These injunctions to refrain from certain arbitrary coercions are properly called the Bill of Rights.

Today, the government of the United States is founded on the principle that there are certain things it *must do* for the people: These prescriptions to provide for health and welfare ought properly to be called the Bill of Wrongs.

Americans now expect physicians (or their surrogates)

to bring them into the world; teach them how to live in it; cure them when they fall ill; prevent them from harming themselves or others (and prevent others from harming them); and kill them when they are old (an act which they mistakenly conceptualize as 'euthanasia'). The more physicians fulfill these expectations, the unhappier people, as patients, become with the medical profession. Why? Because, not surprisingly, the patient's expectations are fulfilled on terms set by physicians and the State, not by the patient.

When a child in a family of Christian Scientists dies without medical attendance, say of meningitis, his parents are prosecuted for manslaughter or child-neglect. At the same time, the Federal Government recognizes Christian Science as a legitimate method of healing, exemplified by the following statement in the 1989 edition of *The Medicare Handbook*: "Medical hospital insurance can help pay for inpatient hospital and skilled nursing facility services you receive in a participating Christian Science sanatorium if it is operated or listed and certified by the First Church of Christ, Scientist, in Boston."[4] This passage, headed "Care in a Christian Science Sanatorium," revealingly appears next to, and on the same page as, the passage headed "Care In A Psychiatric Hospital".

The moral: having assumed the role of determining what is, and what is not, effective or legitimate treatment for disease, the American government has decreed that faith healing is a species of scientific healing, thus abolishing the fundamental distinction between ceremonial and technical performances.

Medical care — that is, being in a hospital as a patient or receiving treatment from a physician — may itself be the cause of a whole class of illnesses, aptly called 'iatrogenic'. Clearly, one of the important medical advances that still lies ahead of us is the control of iatrogenic diseases. I surmise that this therapeutic breakthrough — pioneered by psychiatrists in their epoch-making discovery of deinstitutionalization — will consist of physicians recommending — if necessary, requiring — patients to stay away from hospitals and doctors and defining the policy as a type of therapy. Non-hospitalization (formerly called 'staying at home') and non-treatment (formerly called 'taking good care of oneself') will thus be added to the scientific physician's therapeutic armamentarium. The use of these medical interventions will, of course, be restricted to members of the medical profession who will charge appropriate fees for dispensing these invaluable therapeutic services.

People are free in proportion as the State protects them from *others*; and are oppressed in proportion as the State protects them from *themselves*. "Look to the State for nothing beyond law and order," wrote Frederic Bastiat. "Count on it for no wealth, no enlightenment."[5] Yet it is conventional wisdom today that we ought to look to the State for protection from drugs, mental illness, and suicide — in short, from our own choices and their consequences.

Epitaph for the Therapeutic State:

"Well then, maybe it would be worth mentioning the

three periods of history. When man believed that happiness was dependent upon God, he killed for religious reasons. When he believed that happiness was dependent upon the form of government, he killed for political reasons . . .

After dreams that were too long, true nightmares . . . we arrived at the present period of history. Man woke up, discovered that which he always knew, that happiness is dependent upon health, and began to kill for therapeutic reasons. . . .

When no one believed any longer in the politicians, it was medicine, with its amazing discoveries, that captured the imagination of the human race. It is medicine that has come to replace both religion and politics in our time."[6]

SOURCES

Epigram

* *The Holy Bible*, Revised Standard Version (New York: Meridian, 1964), p. 214.

Preface

[1] Jacques Barzun, *Science: The Glorious Entertainment* (New York: Harper & Row, 1964), pp. 191–226.

[2] Albert Camus, *The Plague* (1947), translated by Stuart Gilbert (New York: Modern Library, 1948), p. 121.

Introduction

[1] Voltaire, quoted in Victor Thaddeus, *Voltaire: Genius of Mockery* (New York: Brentano's 1928), p. 214; and quoted in Jean Orieux, *Voltaire*, translated by Barbara Bray and Helen R. Lane (Garden City, NY: Doubleday, 1979), p. 461.

[2] James, 4:9, *The Holy Bible*, Revised Standard Version (New York: Meridian, 1964), p. 215.

[3] Francis Bacon, *Essays* (1597), quoted in Burton Stevenson, ed., *The Macmillan Book of Proverbs, Maxims, and Famous Phrases*, (New York: Macmillan, 1948), p. 1265.

⁴ Mikhail Bakhtin, *Rabelais and His World* (1965), translated by Helene Iswolsky (Bloomington: Indiana University Press, 1984), p. 73.

⁵ Rabelais, quoted in ibid., p. 69.

⁶ Bakhtin, ibid., pp. 94–95.

⁷ Voltaire, quoted in Victor Thaddeus, op. cit., p. 235.

DISEASE

¹ Chris A. Raymond, 'Political Campaign Pinpoints "Stigma Hurdle" Facing Nation's Mental Health Community', *Journal of the American Psychiatric Association*, 260: 1338 (September 9), 1988.

² Joyce Fairbairn, 'A Senator's Lament: "Too Many Canadians Cannot Read the Charter of Rights",' *Whig-Standard* (Kingston, Ontario), September 16, 1987, p. 11.

³ Norm Ovenden, 'Southam Literacy Survey Contains Unsettling News for Newspaper Industry', ibid., September 17, 1987, p. 10. (I wish to thank Mark Barnes for providing these two items.)

⁴ Quoted in, 'Sexual Behavior Likened to Addiction', *Washington Post*, April 2, 1988, p. C11.

⁵ Jim Fuller, 'Physician Offers Hope for Adulterers and Their Spouses', *Syracuse Post-Standard*, May 9, 1988, p. A14.

⁶ Quoted in Bill Stokes, 'Gambling is Being Treated as a Disease', *Buffalo News*, March 29, 1988, p. C7.

⁷ Daniel Goleman, 'Biology of Brain May Hold Key for Gamblers: When the Casino Becomes an Addiction, the Condition may be Chemical', *New York Times*, October 3, 1989, p. C1.

⁸ Lionel Solursh, 'Combat Addiction: Post-Traumatic Stress Disorder Re-explored', *Psychiatric Journal of the University of Ottawa*, 13: 17–20 (March), 1988, p. 20.

⁹ 'Great Works of Art Pose Health Threats to Tourists', *Syracuse Post-Standard*, July 26, 1989, p. D1.

¹⁰ 'Hospital Plans to Wean Teens from Satanism', *Arkansas Democrat*, September 7, 1989, p. 3A.

DRUGS

¹ Harry Anderson et al., 'The Global Poison Trade', *Newsweek*, November 7, 1988, pp. 66–68; p. 68.

² 'Addiction is a Family Problem, Too', *New York Times*, March 20, 1988, p. 50.

³ Edward I. Koch, Advertisement, *New York Times*, March 1, 1988, p. 87.

⁴ Edward I. Koch, 'Welfare Isn't a Way of Life' (Op-ed), *New York Times*, March 4, 1988, p. A39.

⁵ 'Candidates' Survival Guide', *Newsweek*, March 28, 1988, p. 33.

⁶ 'Partnership for a Drug-Free America, "Sometimes . . . " ' (Advertisement), *Newsweek*, April 11, 1988.

⁷ Revelation, 13:10, *The Holy Bible*, Revised Standard Version (New York: Meridian, 1964), p. 235.

⁸ Samuel Butler, *Erewhon* (1872) (Harmondsworth: Penguin, 1954), p. 193.

⁹ This attribution is apocryphal. See Tom Burnam, *The Dictionary of Misinformation*, (New York: Ballantine Books, 1975), pp. 129–130.

ETHICS

¹ Immanuel Kant, quoted in Isaiah Berlin, *Four Essays on Liberty* (London: Oxford University Press 1969), p. 137.

² Shaw, G. B., 'Marxism for Revolutionists' (1903), quoted in Burton Stevenson, ed., *The Macmillan Book of Proverbs, Maxims, and Famous Phrases* (New York: Macmillan, 1948), p. 1899.

³ Barbara W. Tuchman, 'A Nation in Decline?' *New York Times Magazine*, September 20, 1987, pp. 52–56 & 142–145; p. 142.

⁴ See Thomas S. Szasz, *Law, Liberty, and Psychiatry: An Inquiry Into the Social Uses of Mental Health Practices* (New York: Macmillan, 1963), pp. 3–4.

⁵ G. Brock Chisholm, 'The Psychiatry of Enduring Peace and Social

Progress, *Psychiatry*, 9:3–11 (Jan.), 1946: p. 9. During the war, Chisholm was director-general of medical services in the Canadian army; after the war, he became the first director of the United Nation's World Health Organization.

Insanity Defense

[1] Arnold W. Green, 'The Reified Villain', *Social Research*, 35: 656–664 (Winter), 1968; p. 664.

[2] Jacques Barzun, *Science: The Glorious Entertainment* (New York: Harper & Row, 1964), p. 223.

[3] 'North's Motivation Irrelevant, Prosecutors Say', *Syracuse Herald-Journal*, March 8, 1989, p. A4.

[4] Sir Hartley Shawcross, *Trial of the Major War Criminals Before the International Military Tribunal*, Nuremberg, Germany. Proceedings, 19 July–29 July 1946, Vol. XIX, July 26, 1946, p. 467.

Language

[1] Aristotle, 'De Poetica' (Poetics), translated by Ingram Bywater, in Richard McKean, ed., *The Basic Works of Aristotle* (New York: Random House, 1941), p. 1479.

[2] Henry John Temple Palmerston (1784–1865), British foreign secretary, home secretary, and prime minister; quoted in Roland N. Stromberg, *Arnold J. Toynbee: History for an Age in Crisis* (Carbondale, Illinois: Southern Illinois University Press, 1972), p. 102.

[3] 'Jackson and Others Say "Blacks" is Passé', *New York Times*, December 21, 1988, p. A16.

[4] George Steiner, 'K' (1963), in *Language and Silence: Essays on Language, Literature and the Inhuman* (New York: Atheneum, 1967), p. 123.

[5] Jean-Paul Sartre, *Being and Nothingness: An Essay on Phenomenological Ontology* (1943), translated by Hazel E. Barnes (New York: Philosophical Library, 1956), p. 51.

Law

1 M. Grogan, 'Law Limiting Condom Sales Called Obsolete in the '80s', *Syracuse Post-Standard*, July 26, 1989, p. A1.

Legitimacy

1 Abigail Van Buren, 'Husband's Behavior at Wake Irks Minister', *Syracuse Post-Standard*, July 11, 1987, p. A8.

2 Wally Hall, 'Another Example of Drug Abuse Problem', *Arkansas Democrat*, July 19, 1987, p. C-1. Bill Brown, a former Arkansan and head coach at Sacramento State College, was arrested for possession of cocaine and fired from his job.

3 Quoted in Jean Orieux, *Voltaire*, translated by Barbara Bray and Helen R. Lane (Garden City, NY: Doubleday, 1979), p. 284.

Liberty

1 Bill Keller, 'Polling Moscow: Western-style Survey Finds Residents Disapprove of Freeing Dissidents', *Syracuse Herald-Journal*, November 2, 1987, p. A-12.

2 I speak here of personal freedom, not political liberty. It is the latter which both Montesquieu and Kant mistakenly equated with 'the power of doing what we ought to will'. See Isaiah Berlin, *Four Essays on Liberty* (London: Oxford University Press, 1969), p. 147.

3 See Robert W. Poole, Jr., 'Things are a Lot Groovier Now', *Reason*', May 1988, pp. 48–49.

Medicine

1 'Schizophrenia Drug OK'd', *American Medical News*, October 20, 1989, p. 51.

Mental Illness

1 Flyer, McGill Law Conference, March 26, 1986.

2 Ludwig Wittgenstein, *Culture and Value*, edited by G. H. von Wright, translated by Peter Winch (Chicago: University of Chicago Press, 1981), p. 54.

3 Ann Japenga, 'Ordeal of Postpartum Psychosis', *Los Angeles Times*, February 1, 1987, Part VI, pp. 1 and 4.

4 'Court Holds Bipolar Disorder is Physical', *Psychiatric News*, 23:16–17 (March 4), 1988.

5 Thomas Hobbes, *Leviathan* (1651), Michael Oakeshott, ed. (New York: Macmillan/Collier, 1962), p. 62.

6 Samuel Butler, *The Way of All Flesh* (1903) (Baltimore: Penguin, 1953), p. 278.

Myth of Mental Illness

1 Stacy V. Jones, 'Patents: Chemical for Diagnosis of Mental Ailments', *New York Times*, January 2, 1988, p. B17.

Personal Conduct

1 'Dismissed Alcoholic Worker Ruled a Victim of Handicap', *New York Times*, March 4, 1988, p. B9.

Politics

1 This is nothing new. In 1843, the Marquis de Custine observed: "The political state of Russia may be defined in one sentence: it is a country in which the government says what it pleases, because it alone has the right to speak . . . " Quoted in Tibor Szamuely, *The Russian Tradition*, Robert Conquest, ed., (New York: McGraw-Hill, 1974), p. 3.

² Thomas Jefferson, 'Notes on the State of Virginia' (1781), in Adrienne Koch and William Peden, eds., *The Life and Selected Writings of Thomas Jefferson* (New York: Modern Library, 1944), p. 276.

³ Thomas Jefferson, 'Inauguration Address, March 4, 1801', in H. A. Washington, ed., *The Writings of Thomas Jefferson* (Philadelphia: Lippincott, 1871), Vol. VIII, Part II, pp. 1–5; p. 3.

PSYCHIATRY

¹ Randolph Bourne, *The Radical Will: Selected Writings, 1911–1918* (New York: Urizen Books, 1977), p. 360.

² Antonin Artaud, 'Van Gogh, the Man Suicided by Society' (1947), In, Susan Sontag, ed., *Antonin Artaud: Selected Writings*, translated by Helen Weaver (New York: Farrar, Straus and Giroux, 1976), p. 496–97.

³ Vincent Van Gogh, *Dear Theo: The Autobiography of Vincent Van Gogh*, Irving Stone, ed., (New York: Signet/New American Library, 1937), pp. 418, 421, 425.

⁴ Lewis L. Judd, quoted in Ronald Kotulak, 'Brain Storms: Phenomenal Advances in Medicine Peeling Away the Secrets of the Mind', *Syracuse Herald-Journal*, May 23, 1988, pp. B1 and B3; p. B3.

⁵ 'Surviving Spouses' Depression Studied', *American Medical News*, February 3, 1989, p. 37.

⁶ Voltaire, quoted in Jean Orieux, *Voltaire*, translated by Barbara Bray and Helen R. Lane (Garden City, NY: Doubleday, 1979), p. 349.

⁷ Kenneth Minogue, *Alien Powers: The Pure Theory of Ideology* (New York: St. Martin's Press, 1985), p. 5.

⁸ 'The Soviets Respond', *Psychiatric News*, 24: 21 (August 4), 1989.

PSYCHOANALYSIS

¹ Sigmund Freud, Letter to Wilhelm Fliess, February 1, 1890, in Jeffrey Moussaieff Masson, ed., *The Complete Letters of Sigmund Freud to Wilhelm Fliess, 1887–1904* (Cambridge: Harvard University Press, 1985), p. 398.

² Anna Freud, Letter to Sigmund Freud, July 20, 1922, Freud Collection,

Library of Congress, quoted in Peter Gay, *Freud: A Life for Our Time* (New York: Norton, 1988), p. 438.

3 Sigmund Freud, Letter to Wilhelm Fliess, February 4, 1888, in Jeffrey Moussaieff Masson, ed., *The Complete Letters of Sigmund Freud to Wilhelm Fliess, 1887–1904* (Cambridge: Harvard University Press, 1985), p. 18.

4 Sigmund Freud, Letter to Marie Bonaparte, August 13, 1937, in *Letters of Sigmund Freud*, edited by Ernst L. Freud, translated by Tania and James Stern (New York: Basic Books, 1960), p. 436.

PSYCHOTHERAPY

1 See Stefan Zweig, *Mental Healers: Franz Anton Mesmer, Mary Baker Eddy, Sigmund Freud* [1932], translated by Eden and Cedar Paul (New York: Frederic Ungar, 1962).

2 Samuel Butler, *The Way of All Flesh* (1903) (London: Penguin, 1950).

3 Joseph Breuer and Sigmund Freud, *Studies on Hysteria* (1893–95), in James Strachey, ed., *The Standard Edition of the Complete Psychological Works of Sigmund Freud* (London: Hogarth, 1955), Vol. II.

4 Samuel Butler, *The Way of All Flesh*, pp. 214–15.

5 Sigmund Freud, 'Postscript to the Question of Lay Analysis' (1927), *Standard Edition*, Vol. XX, pp. 255–56.

6 Voltaire, *Philosophical Dictionary*, Theodore Besterman, ed., and trans. (Harmondsworth: Penguin, 1971), p. 289.

PUNISHMENT

1 Hank Briody, 'Ask the Incarcerated about the Death Penalty' (Letters), *New York Times*, September 13, 1987, p. E34.

RELIGION

1 Geoffrey Parrinder, ed., *World Religions: From Ancient History to the Present* (New York: Facts on File, 1983), p. 488.

SCHIZOPHRENIA

1 'Embryos and Parkinson's Disease' (Editorial), *The Lancet*, 1: 1077, 1: 1087 (May 14), 1988.

2 Thomas S. Szasz, *Insanity: The Idea and Its Consequences* (New York: Wiley, 1987), p. 365.

3 J. Story, *Commentaries on the Constitution of the United States* [1833] (Book III, chap. XLIV, para. 1877), quoted in Miller, G. T., *Religious Liberty in America: History and Prospects* (Philadelphia: Westminster Press, 1976), p. 77.

4 Quoted in Christopher Cerf and Victor Navasky, eds., *The Experts Speak: A Definitive Compendium of Authoritative Misinformation* (New York: Pantheon, 1984), pp. 69–70.

5 'How Families and Professionals Can Work Together as Partners', *AMI* (Alliance for the Mentally Ill of New York State), March 1989, pp. 3–4; p. 4.

6 Myre Sim, 'Organic or Functional?', *Proceedings of the Royal College of Physicians of Edinburgh*, 17: 232–246 (October), 1987; p. 233.

7 See Kenneth Minogue, *Alien Powers: The Pure Theory of Ideology*, (New York: St. Martin's Press, 1985).

SEX

1 With acknowledgment to Ambrose Bierce, who defines marriage as "The state or condition of a community consisting of a master, a mistress, and two slaves, making in all two." Ambrose Bierce, *The Devil's Dictionary* (1911) (New York: Dover, 1958), p. 86.

SUICIDE

1 'Lawyers Back Aid in Suicide', *New York Times*, September 23, 1987, p. D30.

THERAPEUTIC STATE

[1] Robin Norwood, quoted in 'Getting Beyond Mr. Wrong', *San Francisco Chronicle*, February 26, 1988, p. E14.

[2] Quoted, with approval, in V. Herzlich and J. Pierret, *Illness and Self in Society* (1984), translated by Elborg Forster (Baltimore: Johns Hopkins University Press, 1987), p. 231.

[3] Jeffrey Schmalz, 'Cuomo's Health Chief: Innovation and Influence', *New York Times*, March 4, 1988, pp. B1 & B4.

[4] U.S. Department of Health and Human Services, *The Medicare Handbook* (Baltimore: Health Care Financing Administration, Publication No. HCFA 10050), 1980, p. 10.

[5] Frederic Bastiat, quoted in George C. Roche, *Frederic Bastiat: A Man Alone* (New Rochelle, NY: Arlington House, 1971), p. 164.

[6] Adolfo Bioy Casares, 'Plans for an Escape to Carmelo', *New York Review of Books*, April 10, 1986, p. 7.